Forts and Castles
of Ghana

Albert van Dantzig

Forts and Castles of Ghana

Sedco Publishing Limited

Sedco Publishing Limited
Accra

ISBN   9964   72   010   6

Printers: Commercial Associates Ltd., Accra.

Contents

List of Illustrations

Introduction

The coat of arms of the Republic of Ghana shows among other things a little fort. This is not without significance: the numerous forts and castles along Ghana's shores have played an important role in her history. These structures, built by various European nations to protect their trade on the 'Guinea Coast', are still today one of Ghana's most striking features.

Tradeposts, fortified or not, have been built in various parts of the world, but nowhere in such great numbers along such a relatively short stretch of coast. At various places, such as Accra, Kómenda and Sekondi, forts were actually built within gun-range of each other. Within three centuries more than sixty castles, forts and lodges were built along a stretch of coast less than 300 miles (500 km) long. Many of these buildings are still in existence at the present, and if some of them could be regarded as important individual monuments, the whole chain of buildings, whether intact, ruined or merely known as sites, could be seen as a *collective historical monument* unique in the world: the ancient 'shopping street' of West Africa. The 'shops' varied greatly in size and importance. If some could be compared with department stores, others were hardly more than village stores.

The appellation *castle* is applied only to the three biggest of these buildings: Elmina Castle, Cape Coast Castle and Christiansborg Castle, the former headquarters of respectively the Portuguese (later of the Dutch), the British and the Danes. *Fort* is applied to the larger fortified buildings, and *lodge* to small trade-factories, sometimes virtually unfortified. Of the latter only very few traces are left here and there; sometimes they were simple mud-huts with at best one or two cannon to defend them, sometimes less, like the *'logie'* the Dutch had in the late seventeenth century on 'Mount Congh' (Queen Anne's Point): according to a contemporary report the Dutch West India Company had that tradepost guarded by a mere 'man armed with an axe'! To our knowledge the following list of castles, forts and lodges – from west to east – could be regarded as complete:

1 Fort St Louis; wooden French fort at Assini (Ivory Coast, near Ghana border), built in 1698, abandoned 1704. No traces at present.
2 Fort Apollonia at Beyin. Built by British 1756. 1868–1872 Dutch and known as Fort William III. At present a resthouse.
3 Swedish (later Dutch) lodge at Jumore: second half seventeenth century. No traces.
4 Portuguese, later Dutch 'Toll House' at mouth of Ankobra river. Probably on site of present ticket office for Ankobra Ferry.
5 Dutch lodge 'Elize Carthago' on 'Mount Ankober', the hill overlooking the left bank of the mouth of the Ankobra. Early eighteenth century. It was intended to extend it into a fort, and at one stage fourteen iron guns were brought on top of the hill, but the plan was never executed. Few traces.
6 Portuguese fort at confluence of Ankobra and Duma rivers, near present Ankobra bridge, built 1623(?) to guard gold-mine at Akwaso or Dwete-bo, but soon abandoned. A few traces(?).
7 Dutch fort or lodge 'Ruychaver' at Old Awudua, on right bank of Ankobra, about 10 miles (16 km) south of present Prestea, built 1654, blown up 1659. A few traces still visible.
8 Portuguese fort S. Antonio, built at Axim 1515(?), a little to the east of an earlier fort. Dutch 1642–1872. At present in use as post office, various government offices.
9 Fort Gross Friedrichsburg at Princes Town (Pokesu), built 1683 by Brandenburgers. 1717–25 in hands of John Conny. 1725–1872 Dutch, known as Fort Hollandia. At

present in use as residence for nurses of German hospital.

10 Brandenburg lodge Louisa at Takrama, 1685. Taken over by Dutch 1717, but probably soon abandoned. No traces(?).

11 Brandenburg fort Dorothea at Akwida, built 1687. Taken over by Dutch in 1717. Abandoned in later eighteenth century. At present a ruin.

12 English fort at Dixcove, built 1693. 1868–72 Dutch and known as Fort Metalen Kruis. At present a resthouse.

13 Butri: Swedish lodge 1650, soon abandoned. Dutch fort 'Batensteyn' 1656, abandoned in the late nineteenth century. At present under reconstruction.

14 Takoradi: Dutch, Swedish, Brandenburg, English and French lodges late seventeenth century. Dutch fort 'Witsen' built 1656, blown up in 1665, but later rebuilt. No known traces at present.

15 Sekondi: Dutch fort 'Oranje', built 1690 on foundations of lodge (1642). At present in use by Ghana Railway and Ports Authority as a lighthouse.

16 Sekondi: English fort, built 1682; few traces at present.

17 Shama: Portuguese fort S. Sebastião, built 1523. Bombarded and rebuilt by Dutch 1640. At present in use as post office and government offices.

18 Komenda: British fort, built 1687, Dutch 1868–72, now a ruin. French lodge built and destroyed 1687.

19 Dutch Komenda (Kankan): fort 'Vreedenburgh', built 1682 on foundation of lodge. Now a ruin.

20 Elmina: Castle S. Jorge, built by Portuguese 1482, Dutch headquarters 1637–1872. Fort Coenraadsburg, built 1665 on top of S. Iago Hill, on site of former (1637) fortification. Nineteenth century fortifications: a) 'Veersche Schans' (near Bantama); b) 'Beeckesteyn' (near lagoon); c) 'Schomerus' (formerly 'Coebergh') on site of present St Joseph school; d) 'Java' (formerly 'Cattoenbergh') on 'Java-hill', traces visible; e) 'Nagtglas', near eastern entrance route of Elmina, no traces; and f) watchtower (still standing in Government Garden).

21 Cape Coast: Swedish fort 'Carolusburg' (1653), 1661–64 in hands of 'Dey' of Fetu, 1664–65 Dutch, 1665

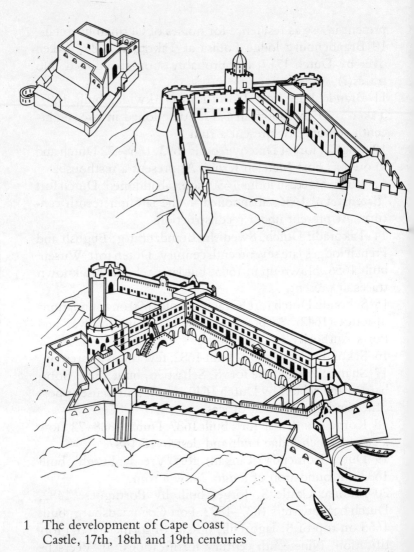

1 The development of Cape Coast
Castle, 17th, 18th and 19th centuries

British and extended into Cape Coast Castle, British headquarters up to 1876. Now houses West African Historical
Museum. Cape Coast 'out-forts': a) Phipps' Tower
(1721); b) Fort William; and c) Fort Victoria. The latter
two are nineteenth century and well preserved.
22 Cape Coast/Amanful ('Manfro'): Danish fort 'Fredriksborg' 1661, sold to British 1679. Later reconstructed and
known as 'Fort Royal'. Few traces at present.

23 Mount Congh or Queen Anne's Point: Dutch, later English lodges, from second half seventeenth century. No traces.

24 Mori: Fort 'Nassau', Dutch headquarters 1612–37; English 1868. Now a ruin.

25 Biriwa or Anashan: English fort (1673). No traces(?).

26 Egya: English and Dutch lodges in seventeenth and eighteenth centuries.

27 Anomabu: Dutch fort 1630–64. English fort 'Charles' built 1674, abandoned in 1730s, rebuilt 1756, and extended in nineteenth century when it became known as Fort William; at present in use as prison.

28 The French had a fort at Anomabu 1754–58. No traces.

29 Kormantin/Abandze: Former English headquarters (1631–65). After capture by Dutch known as Fort 'Amsterdam'. English 1868. Now a ruin. Conservation in progress.

30 French fort at Amoku, near Saltpond: 1787–1807. Few traces left.

31. English fort at Tantumquery: built 1702 (as a lodge?); extended 1721. Few traces left at present.

32 Legu: English and Danish lodges (seventeenth and eighteenth centuries); no traces known at present.

33 Apam: Dutch fort 'Leydsaemheyt' (Patience), built 1698–1704. English 1868. At present a resthouse.

34 Dutch lodge at Winnebah, later English, and 1673 extended into a fort. Bombarded 1812. Few traces still visible in Methodist Church building.

35 Senya Beraku: Dutch fort 'De Goede Hoop' (Good Hope), built 1702, later extended. English 1868. Now under reconstruction.

36 Shidoe: English lodge, early eighteenth century. No traces(?).

37 Nyinyanu: Dutch lodge, eighteenth century. No traces(?).

38 Accra: Portuguese lodge on promontory near modern Brazil Lane. No traces.

39 Accra: Dutch fort 'Crèvecoeur', built 1649 on site of earlier lodge, largely destroyed in 1863 earthquake. Handed over to English in 1868, and since then known as Ussher

Fort. At present a prison.

40 Accra: James Fort, built 1673. At present a prison.

41 Accra/Osu: Christiansborg Castle, built 1661 onwards by Danes. 1681–83 in Portuguese hands and known as Fort S. Francisco Xavier. 1693 in hands of Akwamu. 1850 sold to British. Since 1876 seat of government.

42 Labadi: Dutch and Danish lodges, eighteenth century. No traces.

43 Teshi: Dutch and Danish lodges, eighteenth century, 1783 Danish fort Augustaborg. Few traces at present.

44 Dutch lodge, later fort, at Tema (1701, 1714). No traces left.

45 Dutch lodge at Kpone (1701–?). Few traces.

46 Prampram: English fort Vernon, built 1745(?). Few traces in walls of modern resthouse.

47 Old Ningo: Danish fort 'Fredensborg', built 1734. English 1850. At present a ruin.

48 Tubreku: eighteenth century Danish lodge. No traces.

49 Ada: Fort Kongensten, built 1783. English 1850. Few traces at present.

50 Keta: Dutch fort 'Singelenburgh', built 1734, blown up 1737. Dutch and Danish lodges afterwards. Danish fort 'Prindsensten' built 1784. English 1850. At present a prison.

The essential purpose of all these buildings was to serve as store-houses for goods brought from Europe and bought on the Coast, and as living quarters for a permanent commercial and military staff. If the earliest of these buildings were mainly fortified on the land-side against enemies expected from that side, soon the real danger appeared to come rather from the side of the sea, in the form of European competitors. During the sixteenth century a growing number of French and English ships came to trade in what was supposed to be a Portuguese monopoly area. An even more serious threat to Portuguese supremacy on the Coast came from the Dutch, who had arrived in large numbers on the coast by the end of that century. In 1612 they built a fort of their own at Mori after the local chief of Asebu, who had for some time been trading with them, had sent two ambassadors on one of their ships to the Netherlands with the request that a fort be built in his state. This was the first of a long line of forts which were in fact only built for the sake of keeping a foothold on the coast and of driving competitors away. Within a few decades several European nations had jumped on the bandwagon and by 1700 the majority of the forts as we now know them had been built.

It should be pointed out that the Europeans did not have any territorial jurisdiction beyond the walls of their forts; the very land on which they were built was only rented. Each European nation tried to reserve exclusive trading rights for itself with the local rulers. It is therefore not surprising that political disintegration set in all along the coast, and consequently the tradeposts had to be armed not only to drive competitors away, but also to protect the traders inside the forts or the people on whose territory they were built against attacks by neighbouring African states.

It was also for geographical reasons that all this European commercial activity concentrated in this relatively small area: first of all there is the obvious fact that Ghana is the only area where there are substantial gold deposits comparatively near to the coast. But Ghana's coast is also suitable for building forts because it is rocky, thus providing building material and strong natural foundations, and access from the interior to the sea is not, as in neighbouring areas, interrupted by lagoons and mangrove swamps. One may contend that forts were also built at Whydah on the 'Slave Coast', on the landward side of a lagoon, but these forts could not stand comparison with those of the Gold Coast: they had mud walls and only a few cannon, which were used mainly for the firing of salutes: the sea-roads were beyond the reach of those guns. The King of Whydah, and later the King of Dahomey, maintained absolute power over their European 'guests'. In 1703 the King of Whydah even imposed a unique treaty on the European traders who had settled in his state: in spite of the war they were fighting in their 'Christian Empire' (the War of the Spanish Succession) they were to live in peace and harmony in his state and not to attack each other's ships on the Whydah roads, thus spoiling his lucrative slave-trade.

A further advantage of Ghana's irregular, rocky coast was the fact that it has a number of natural harbours in the form of coves or bays and capes, while other parts cannot be approached because of dangerous rocky reefs. Consequently ships had to concentrate in definite areas for trade, which could be commanded from the tops of the promontories on which many of these forts were built. Low sandy beaches are much more difficult to check, as trade contacts can be established anywhere along them. Only at the very end of the fort-building period were two forts built in such areas: the English one at Beyin in Nzima, and the Danish one at the opposite end of the coast on the Keta peninsula.

The history of the forts and castles of Ghana could be considered as part of 'colonial history' in the sense of being part of the history of European overseas expansion. But it is not the history of suppression of liberty and exploitation as much of colonial history is. Nearly all the forts were built with the consent, sometimes at the urgent request, of the local chiefs and people. It would be wrong to idealise the relationship between Africans and Europeans in those days, but it cannot be denied that they traded with each other basically on a footing of equality. More often than not they tried to cheat each other, but it was done with equanimity. The forts were built to keep other European traders away, and it was on the side of the sea that they had their strongest defence. It cannot be denied that on a few occasions guns of the forts were trained on the houses of what the Europeans misleadingly called their 'subject natives', but in such brawls these 'subjects' invariably proved to be 'over-mighty': without their co-operation the Europeans in the forts could not survive.

Without the forts and castles the history of Ghana would have been very different. Ghanaians, at least those on the coast, but also many in the interior, had had more than 300 years to get to know Europeans as their equals in their dealings at the forts before the real 'colonial' era of the nineteenth and twentieth centuries. This was bound to have a great influence on the attitudes of the people of Ghana who are justly famed for their open-mindedness towards the outside world.

The history of the construction of the various castles, forts and lodges along the coast of Ghana thus covers a period of more than 300 years, which can be roughly sub-divided as follows:

1 the period of Portuguese hegemony, 1470–1600
2 that of Dutch and English penetration, 1600–40
3 that of keen competition between various companies, 1640–1710
4 that of relatively peaceful co-existence between companies, 1710–1800
5 that of early colonisation, 1800–1900

During the long first period only one castle, two forts and (possibly) one lodge were built; during the second, two forts and one or two lodges were added; but during the seventy years which followed we see several waves of intensive constructional activity: no less than two castles, twenty-two forts and a large number of lodges were built; during the fourth period only four or five forts and a few lodges were built, while the last period saw the construction of only a few military fortifications and the gradual decay of a number of old tradeposts.

In the present century the surviving forts and castles have served, and are still serving, a wide variety of purposes. Christiansborg Castle has remained since 1876 Ghana's seat of government; Elmina Castle, for a long time in use as a police training depot, may one day be converted into a big tourist hostel; Cape Coast Castle has become a West African historical museum. Various forts are in use as – or are being converted into – resthouses; some forts house post offices and other public facilities, others are being used as prisons. It is the policy of the Ghana Museums and Monuments Board to make all these monuments fully accessible to the public and to restore them in the most authentic style.

1 The period of Portuguese monopoly

The Gold Coast, former name of Ghana, really was quite an appropriate name for this coast in the days when these forts were built; apart from Latin America, monopoly of Spain, West Africa was the only major supplier of gold in those days. Certainly, Europe has had its own gold-mines, but by the time of the Renaissance, when the European economy went through a period of fast expansion and the entire financial system was based on the possession of gold, most of these mines were exhausted or fell into the hands of the Muslim Turkish Empire.

Gold from Africa was already known to Europeans before their voyages of reconnaissance of the fifteenth century; considerable quantities of this gold had crossed the Mediterranean from North Africa, in particular into the Muslim southern half of the Iberian peninsula, the Caliphate of Cordoba. Many traders, especially Italians, travelled to North Africa, and towards the end of the fifteenth century one of them, Benedetto Dei of Genoa, reported on his visit to the fabulously rich city of Timbuktu in Songhai, where he saw that even the collars of the king's dogs were made of gold.

Italy, cradle of the renaissance civilisation and centre of the Mediterranean world, remained politically, however, utterly divided. It fell to the monarchy of one of the first European nation-states, Portugal, on the shores of the Atlantic, to sponsor the little fleets which, making use of the newly developed navigational techniques, were to initiate the 'Age of Discovery'. Prince Henry 'the Navigator', nephew of King John I of Portugal, had three main motives for encouraging the reconnaissance of the unknown world beyond the Straits of Gibraltar: to establish contact with the legendary 'Prester John', leader of a fabled Christian Empire beyond the 'Mountains of the Moon', and to attack together with him the Muslims in their rear; to transform Lisbon, then still a mere re-distribution market for Asian goods from Venice (which in its turn received these goods via the land-route and many middlemen from India and the Far East) into the terminus of a sea-route round Africa to India; and to gain direct access to the sources of Africa's gold.

Prince Henry would not live to see his first two aims fulfilled. But during his lifetime the first relatively small quantities of 'Guinea gold' were brought to Portugal, together with some slaves, from Senegambia. By the time of his death, in 1460, his explorers had reached the area of Sierra Leone – so named because of the lion-like roars of the frequent thunderstorms there – but from a navigational point of view it looked to them as if they had also reached the limit: there they could at night only dimly see their traditional guiding star, the polar star, just above the horizon.

After the death of their patron, the explorers seemed to be deprived of incentive, but not for long. In 1469 King Alfonso V leased 'the enterprise of Africa' to one Fernão Gomes for five years, on condition that his men explore each year at least 100 leagues of coastline. By the time this contract expired, Gomes' captains had done even better than that and had reached as far as Cape Lopez (Gabon), south of the Equator. In 1471 his men had reached that part of the African coast which seemed to be most promising because of the large quantities of gold which could be obtained there in exchange for relatively little merchandise. The first of such transactions took place at the mouth of the Prah river, the local people possibly selling alluvial gold from the river. As so much gold was offered for sale in this area, the Portuguese thought that the gold-mines must be very near the coast, to which they began to refer as the *Mina de Ouro* or the gold-mine.

News of the discovery of this *Mina de Ouro* soon sread

2

from Portugal to neighbouring Castile. When in 1475 a war broke out between the two countries on account of a succession dispute, the new Queen of Castile, Isabella, formally authorised her subjects to engage in the Guinea trade, in spite of the monopoly which the Pope had earlier granted for that trade to the Portuguese. There ensued several clashes between Portuguese and Castilian ships – or even fleets – along the Guinea coast, but in the end the Portuguese clearly proved stronger. At home, however, they were defeated. The Treaty of Alcaçovas of 1479 recognised Isabella's succession to the throne of Castile, but excluded the Castilians from the Guinea trade. It was the first European treaty to deal with 'colonial spheres of influence'.

The following years, however, demonstrated that the Castilians could not be trusted to obey the treaty to the letter, and soon their ships reappeared all along the coasts of Africa; the Portuguese saw themselves compelled to take other measures to protect their trade, in particular that of the *Mina de Ouro*. There, trade was concentrating on a place the Portuguese called *Aldea das Duas Partes*, the 'Village of Two Parts', situated at the mouth of a little river, or rather lagoon, the Benya, near one of the best natural harbours of the coast. From the shallow lagoon considerable quantities of salt, an important commodity in the trade with the interior, were in those days – as now – extracted. It was here that the Portuguese in 1482 decided to build a major stronghold to protect their trade.

When the Portuguese first arrived, they found the people wearing heavy gold ornaments: long before that, an extensive barter trade in gold and salt must have been in existence at that place. The traders from the interior showed great interest in the new manufactured goods from Portugal, and *a Mina*, as the newcomers called it, soon developed into an important market.

At first the Portuguese proposal to build a castle at Elmina was not over-enthusiastically received: Caramança,[1] the local chief, is said to have retorted, in a very diplomatic way, that the Europeans might not be happy in the place because of the hot climate and the

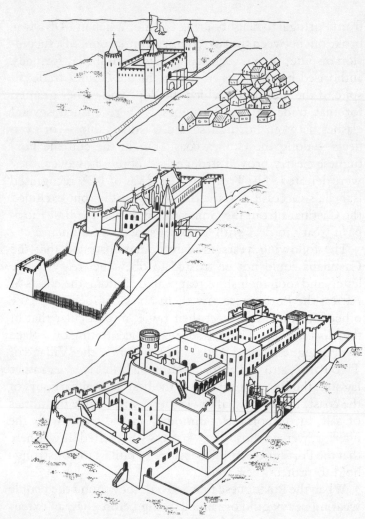

2 The development of Elmina Castle,
   15th, 17th and 19th centuries

difficulty of procuring in his country the luxuries they were
used to in their own, adding that 'the passions that are
common to us all' would inevitably bring on disputes. He
concluded that it would be far preferable for both nations to
continue on the same footing as hitherto, allowing the
Portuguese ships to come and go as usual.

Caramança was quite correct in his presumption that

many Europeans were to die on this coast. Indeed it became notorious as the 'whiteman's grave', more as a result of the highly unhealthy life which the Europeans led in the forts, than as a result of the unhealthiness of the climate; but the disputes which he expected to take place were not all that frequent and did not prevent the rapid growth of commerce.

São Jorge Castle was built in a very short time by a large number of soldiers and craftsmen brought for that purpose from Portugal. Most of the stone for the construction of the castle was quarried from the rocky peninsula on which it stands, the quarry thus forming at the same time a defensive ditch across it. But while these men were at work, they were attacked by the people of Elmina for having disturbed a sacred place. There is still in one of the vaults of the castle a shrine, erected to pacify the spirit of the rock.

Large quantities of red burnt brick were also brought from Portugal to provide the finishing touches to such structures as door and window-arches or rib-vaults.[2] Other building materials, such as mortar, plaster, rafters and beams, which later on would be produced locally, had in 1482 to be imported.

St George's Castle, named after the patron-saint of Portugal, has remained the biggest of all. Even though it has been enlarged several times, its original structure was already quite impressive. It has been suggested that the castle's structure shows similarities to that of the crusaders' castles in the Middle East. At the time they were building it, the Portuguese may still have been thinking along the lines of Ptolemy's maps, which shows a much smaller Africa; the Cape of Good Hope was not discovered until four years later.[3] Elmina Castle may have been built rather as a base for potential campaigns, with or without 'Prester John', against the Infidel, than as the fortified tradepost it became. Indeed, the Portuguese were quite active in their missionary zeal and converted a large number of Elmina's inhabitants to the Christian religion. Fear of an impending Muslim attack may explain the haste with which they built.

The vast castle remained the Portuguese headquarters in

Africa, but soon it was felt that in order to tap the riches of the Gold Coast to the fullest extent other permanent tradeposts were necessary. During the sixteenth century two more forts were built. The most natural choice of sites was the mouths of the Ankobra and Prah rivers, which both run through gold-bearing areas, and in which much panning was done.

Relatively little is known of the long Portuguese period. In the beginning Elmina Castle was probably a high square building with towers on the corners, around a central courtyard – the smallest of the three courtyards of the modern castle – much in the same style as the Tower of London. Of the original corner-towers only the round tower on the north-east, and the half-octagonal tower on the south-west are still in existence; the latter was probably originally round too, as can be seen in a small, odd-shaped and dark room in the mezzanine floor above the main entrance. On the north-west and the south-east were probably at first square towers, but nothing remains of these. At a very early stage the north-western tower must have been replaced by the huge bastion known in the Dutch days as the *Generaelen Battery* because of its proximity to the Director-General's quarters. This bastion, pointing towards the land, forms another indication that the Portuguese expected an attack using sophisticated arms from that side; by the time of the construction of the castle the breach of the walls of Constantinople by the cannon-fire of the 'Infidel' in 1453 was still fresh in the memory of the Christian world, and it seems that the Portuguese were expecting a similar attack in this new Christian outpost. Nonetheless, 150 years later it proved insufficient against such an attack when the Dutch bombarded the castle from the top of St Jago Hill. This bastion, as well as those defending the extensions of the castle on the sea side and the 'French Bastion',[4] was built according to a new design, slightly tapering towards the top, which was more resistant to cannon fire than the original purely vertical towers of the 'keep'. These solid structures could also carry heavier cannon for the defence than the relatively thin towers and curtain-walls. Towards the end of the sixteenth century the Portuguese built within the big new courtyard between the old keep and the sea a new church dedicated to St George, to replace the chapel of S. Iago (St James) built on the hill opposite the Castle, but abandoned after the first Dutch attack of 1597.

Like Elmina Castle, Fort São Antonio at Axim, the second fort the Portuguese built, has its strongest defence works on the land side. It is more or less triangular in shape, following the contours of the cape on which it is built. The Portuguese had at first a little tradepost or fort a little closer

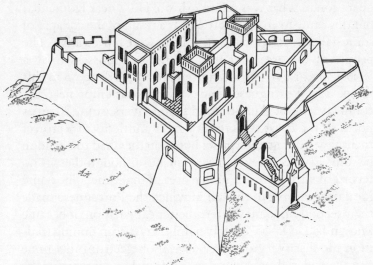

Fort St Anthony, Axim

to the mouth of the Ankobra, but there they were frequently attacked by the people of the neighbouring township of 'Achombene'. The site of the present fort has excellent natural defences in the form of several little rocky islands (on one of which a lighthouse now stands) and dangerous reefs which prevented ships from approaching it closely. Yet, having managed to install cannon on these little islands, the Dutch would later make use of these 'natural defence works' to capture the fort.

Little is known of the original shape of the third Portuguese fort on the Gold Coast, the one at Shama, built about 1550. By the time the Dutch captured it, it was not

7

much more than a ruin, and very little of the present structure seems to be of Portuguese origin. Of the supposed fort or lodge the Portuguese had at Accra, nothing is known but the site, the steep cliff below what is now known as 'Brazil Lane', between Ussher Fort and James Fort, which the Dutch used to call the *'Portugeese Clip'*.

In the 1620s, under the pressure of growing foreign competition, which made the Africans take most of their gold to others, the Portuguese tried to get themselves access to gold-mines in the interior; they are said to have engaged in – or at least to have had a certain interest in – a gold mining operation in what was called 'Abrobi Hill', near Komenda, but this came to an untimely end as a result of the collapse of some galleries in which some miners were buried alive. The people of the area said that the hill was possessed by a *sasabonsam* or evil spirit, and refused to work again in this mine. The Portuguese made a second attempt near the confluence of the Ankobra and Duma rivers, some 20 miles north of the coast, where they built a little fort to protect their new mining enterprise; but soon they had to abandon it: some say because of an earthquake, although there is no record of such an event in that area at that time. The name local people gave to the hill in which the Portuguese made their second mine may offer a better explanation: it became known as *'Dwete-bo'* or 'Silver-hill'; in African mining tradition the discovery of silver (*dwete*) or electrum in a mine was considered a bad omen, and such a site would be abandoned at once.

The historical importance of the Portuguese period lies in particular in the fact that it was then that a *modus vivendi* between Africans and Europeans was evolved which would continue till the nineteenth century. The Europeans did not attempt – as they did in many other parts of the world – to conquer the land or to take possession of it. They contented themselves with remaining mere tenants of the African chiefs to whom they continued to pay ground rents for the land on which they built their forts and a certain subsistence allowance in recognition of their supremacy. Within the walls of the forts, however, the Europeans maintained their own laws and jurisdiction. Elmina, in the days of the Portuguese, assumed a special position: early in the sixteenth century the King of Portugal bestowed upon it the rights of a Portuguese city. As the town straddled the Benya, which formed the border between the Eguafo and Fetu states, there was no strong central leadership, and the townspeople, many of them newcomers, readily accepted the *'regimento da Mina'*, the special code of laws designed for the city. In Axim the Portuguese exercised a kind of informal jurisdiction: there too, African political leadership seems to have lacked unity, and the often quarrelling and relatively powerless chiefs made it their habit to bring their 'palavers' before the commander of Fort São Antonio for arbitration. The Portuguese actively engaged in the conversion of the people around their establishments to the Christian religion. They also levied tolls at various places and even imposed a tax in the form of one fifth of the total catch of fish (and the head of each big fish) to feed the garrisons of the forts in the towns where they settled.

After the Dutch conquest, Elmina seems to have lost its special status. The Dutch recognised the authority of three or more chiefs in the town, to whom they paid ground rent and subsistence allowances. Political contacts between town and castle remained close but informal. At Axim the Dutch claimed 'vassalage by conquest' from the people, but this met with considerable resistance. The (Protestant) Dutch also stopped all missionary activity.

1 The true identity of this 'Caramança' has not yet been fully established and is an issue of considerable historical interest. According to modern local tradition, this name would be derived from 'Kwamena Ansah', a chief of the Eguafo state, in which the south bank of the Benya, on which the castle stands, is situated; but there is also reference to a meeting of Dom Diogo d'Azambuja, the founder of Elmina Castle, with 'Cara Mansa and another Mansa'. 'Mansah' is a Mande word for 'ruler', and it is quite possible that the Portuguese in fact dealt with the chiefs of an established Mandingo community rather than with truly local representatives. Similarly, the name 'Elmina' may be derived from the Arabic *Al-Minah* ('the port'), rather than from the Portuguese word for 'the mine' (*a mina*). A strong Muslim Mandingo presence in the area may also help to explain the effort the Portuguese made to fortify their position in the form of a castle.

2 An example of such rib-vaults can still be seen in the narrow corridor on the east side of the main building, linking the small courtyard with the big one. Samples of Portuguese brick, red and much larger than the generally yellow brick the Dutch

used later, can still be found in the linings of the cisterns below the small court-yard.

3 Christopher Columbus must also have visited Elmina Castle shortly after its foundation when he sailed in the service of the Portuguese. His suggestion to discover a new route to the East Indies by sailing to the west was taken into serious consideration by the Crown of Portugal in 1484. But the Portuguese lost interest in this plan after Dias' discovery of a passage to the Indian Ocean in 1487, and it was not until 1492 that Columbus could execute his plan under the patronage of Isabella of Castile.

4 This bastion, originally built as a quite separate fortification guarding the mouth of the Benya, probably got this name because it was meant to keep the French, who had become serious competitors to the Portuguese by the middle of the sixteenth century, away from the port of Elmina. The name has also given rise to the rather unlikely story that French sailors reached the Guinea Coast long before the Portuguese, and built a fort at Elmina in the fourteenth century, of which only this bastion remained. The origin of this story can be traced back to the French author Villault de Bellefonds, who, with conscious historical falsifications, wanted to establish French 'rights of priority' in the area, quite in style with Louis XIV's contemporary diplomacy based on the findings of the 'Chambres de Réunion' in Europe.

2 The penetration of the Dutch and their expulsion of the Portuguese

After the initial struggle with the Castilians, the Portuguese enjoyed a period of virtual monopoly in their trade on the Gold Coast. It is true that later in the sixteenth century captains of other nations such as France and England came to trade there, which occasioned the Portuguese, as we have seen, to erect the 'French Bastion', which may actually have been built by captured French sailors. But these visits were of a sporadic character and did not pose a serious challenge to the Portuguese position.

But when the Dutch began to compete with them, towards the end of the sixteenth century, they did so in a big way. The people of the Northern Netherlands rose in revolt against their sovereign, Philip II of Spain, in the 1560s, but this did at first not disturb seriously the important trade the Dutch were carrying on with the Iberians, particularly as re-distributors of goods from Spanish and Portuguese ports in Northern Europe. Even when the crowns of Spain and Portugal were united in 1580 under their enemy Philip II, the traditional pattern of trade continued for some time. But when Philip closed his harbours, including the all-important port of Lisbon, to the Dutch in 1594, he more or less compelled them to find their own way to the places of origin of the exotic goods they used to buy there. Immediately a large number of Dutch ships began to swarm out over the oceans, often manned with people who had gained experience in the service of the Spanish and Portuguese.

In 1596 a Dutch captain on his way to Brazil was driven off his course, and landed more or less by accident on the Gold Coast. Although he was for some time imprisoned by the Portuguese, he returned home with a good quantity of gold. In the same year Dutch ships rounded the Cape of Good Hope and returned with the coveted spices from the East Indies. The trade on the East Indies proved so profitable that only six years later a major national enterprise, the chartered United East Indian Company, was set up. But the Dutch Guinea trade, although it appealed perhaps a little less to the imagination than the fabulous East Indian enterprise, grew fast too. Soon more than 20 ships were equipped for that trade every year, and apart from products like ivory, wax, pepper and dye-wood, they brought vast quantities of gold, a commodity of the greatest national importance for a nation of traders, especially for one which was at war. That war came temporarily to an end in 1609, when a twelve-year truce was signed with Spain. The Spanish promised not to interfere with Dutch activities in the Portuguese overseas empire, on condition that the Dutch stayed out of that of the Spanish. The issue of the establishment of a West Indian counterpart of the so successful East Indian Company became one of political strife in the Netherlands between the party which wanted to turn the truce into a permanent peace and the one which wanted to resume war. As the latter party won, the war was resumed and a charter granted to the new company, which, in view of the fact that prevailing winds and currents compelled ships destined to the West Indies first to pass along the west coast of Africa, was also to control the trade in that area.

The States-General of the Republic had recognised the vital importance of the Guinea trade long before the chartering of this General West Indian Company. Naturally, the Portuguese did all they could to keep off the numerous Dutch ships sent by private shipowners or small companies to trade on the Gold Coast, and they frequently attacked Dutch ships. At first the Admiralties of the Republic were ordered to send cruisers regularly to West Africa to protect Dutch commercial interests there – as in fact they would continue to do till the late eighteenth century – but soon the need was felt for a firm foothold on the Gold Coast. In 1611

12

the chief of Asebu, a small state to the East of Elmina where the Dutch had been actively trading for some time, actually sent two ambassadors on board a returning Dutch ship, requesting the government of the new Republic to build a stronghold on his territory. The following year the Admiralty of Amsterdam sent one Calantius with several carpenters and masons on board a ship loaded with a great quantity of bricks to start the construction of the first Dutch fort on the Gold Coast at Mori. It was important that the fort be built quickly, before the Portuguese could interfere with its construction, and most of the building materials were therefore brought from Holland: today the ruins of the fort still show the vast quantities of Dutch brick used for building its walls. Not only the use of brick – nearly all buildings in the Netherlands are made of brick as there is no natural stone to be found in the country, and the masons who built the fort at Mori therefore had no experience of building with other materials – but also the style of the building betray lack of adaptation to the new environment; the high fort was built much after Northern European fashion and always remained particularly notorious for its unhealthy atmosphere and 'foul stagnant air'.

After 1621 the new West India Company took over the fort at Mori from the State and named it after the Stadholders 'Nassau'. In the 1620s the company quickly extended its activities, not only on the Gold Coast, where it claimed exclusive trading rights at places like Anomabu and 'Little Accra',[1] after having established tradeposts there, but even more on the other side of the Atlantic, where it attacked Spanish shipping in the Caribbean and established new colonies in North as well as in South America. If the Dutch farmers' settlements in the Hudson valley were not very successful, their colony 'New Holland', encroaching on Portuguese Brazil, seemed very promising in the 1630s. It was from this Dutch Brazil that its Governor, John Maurice of Nassau, a cousin of the Stadholder, launched in 1637 the final Dutch assault on Elmina.

An earlier attack, in 1625, had ended in a dismal defeat, the Asebu allies of the Dutch failing to establish timely

13

contact with the invaders, but this time more careful preparations were made. It was no longer for gold alone that the Dutch wanted to have a stronger foothold in Africa: 'New Holland' was a sugar-producing colony, and to work the plantations which they had conquered from the Portuguese the Dutch needed great numbers of slaves. In this respect their *volte-face* is remarkable: at first, before they had any plantation colonies, the Dutch Calvinists had maintained a 'holier-than-thou' attitude, strongly condemning the 'popish' practice of using slave-labour, but as soon as they themselves realised the vast profits which could be derived from it, they readily discovered the appropriate texts in the Scriptures to justify it. The conquest of Elmina, Portuguese headquarters in Africa, was meant to be a major milestone in the total destruction of the Portuguese Atlantic empire. The Dutch had no intention of spoiling their profitable gold-trade by encouraging slave-raiding wars on the Gold Coast, and once they had driven the Portuguese out of Elmina, it did not prove very difficult to expel them from slave-supplying areas such as Angola. Although the Dutch soon lost Angola and Brazil again to the Portuguese, they held on to their conquests on the Gold Coast.

By 1637 respect for the Portuguese was so much in decline in the city of Elmina, that the people did little to come to their defence, and they did not even stop the Dutch from installing heavy guns on top of the hill São Iago — where the Portuguese in former days had had a small chapel consecrated to St James — thus allowing them to bombard the castle on its weakest side from a strategic vantage point. After a few days the Portuguese had to surrender. A white stone in front of the castle is said to mark the spot where they handed over the keys to the Dutch. A stone with a Latin inscription in the wall near the main gate commemorates John Maurice of Nassau's capture of the castle. Two other engraved stones in that wall represent the coat of arms of Dom Diogo d'Azambuja, the Portuguese founder of the castle, and that of the Republic of the United Provinces of the Netherlands.

The north side of the castle was rather badly damaged

during the bombardment, and it is there that we find most of the Dutch additions to the Portuguese structure, such as a new bastion to replace the former 'French Bastion',[2] which was now firmly linked with the main structure of the castle by heavy curtain-walls which enclose the third and last courtyard of the castle, the so-called 'cat yard'.[3] The top floor of the western wing of the 'keep' was transformed into a Dutch Reformed church,[4] a much smaller building than the former church of St George in the main courtyard, which was now horizontally divided in two and converted into a 'house of trade' (*huys van Negotie*) on the ground floor with a soldiers' mess above it. On the left side of this building is a big chimney and the open kitchen where food for the garrison was prepared. The façade of the main building on the main court yard was entirely reconstructed by the Dutch and provided with a monumental arched portico. The forged iron balustrade dates from the days of Director-General Pieter Valckenier (1723–7). The 'W' – probably for West Indische Compagnie – is flanked by the family arms of Valckenier and his wife. In the wall below the platform on which this portico stands, a big tombstone is set in masonry; oddly enough it was deprived of its upper part so that the text does not say to whom the monument was dedicated.[5] Other Dutch additions of some interest are the monumental gate in the outer wall leading to the draw-bridge across the moat, and the brick 'compass', in reality a sundial, which were made in 1679 during the tenure of office of Director-General Heerman Abramsz, who wrote that he had it made 'just like the one in the Amsterdam Admiralty House'.

William Bosman, Chief Merchant at Elmina by the end of the seventeenth century and author of the famous *Accurate Description of the Coast of Guinea*, mentions in the second (Dutch) edition of that book that Director-General William De la Palma – about whom he has not much good to say – at least 'greatly beautified' the castle shortly after 1700 and for instance added 'four tower-like ornamental structures' and some warehouses. Of these ornamental structures two can still be seen: the two little towers on the sea-front, also known as 'Prempeh's rooms', because the Asantehene of that name was kept prisoner there by the British in the last years of the nineteenth century. Another rather attractive addition of later years is the oblong room between the Chief Merchant's Tower and the General's Battery with its portico and row of columns which was built in 1806 as a dining and recreational hall for high-ranking officers. It gives a lively touch to the otherwise stern and massive building.

The Dutch did not wait for other nations to follow the example of their tactics in taking Elmina Castle, but built a strong redoubt on top of St Jago Hill, which later, in the 1660s, was transformed into a strong fort, called Coenraadsburg. A stone above the gate shows parts of the names

Fort St Jago
(Coenraadsburg),
Elmina

of the fort and of the Governor who built it, Director-General J. Valckenburgh. The fort, seen from the sea, seems to have been built back to front; it stands behind the Castle and its strongest and biggest bastions do not face the sea but the hills inland: it was from inland that an attack might be expected, although such an attack has never materialised. A partly defaced inscription on the back of the gate in the fort's outer walls tells us that they were built by Director-General Dirck Wilree in the year 1671. The Dutch always kept the fort well-garrisoned and European convicts were sometimes put in its prisons. From the tower and the west bastion signal-flags were hoisted to communicate with ships approaching Elmina.

The building, perched on the high hill, is still quite impressive, but after 1872 some alterations were made which certainly did not contribute to its beauty. The British reduced the height of the tower considerably, while they added three rooms on top of the guard-room and a second floor to the main building. They also disturbed the symmetry of the building by putting gabled roofs on the north-west and south-east bastions.

Coenraadsburg is unique in that it is the only major coastal fort built purely for military reasons. It did not have commercial warehouses, only military quarters. Another interesting feature is the 'ravelin' in front of the fort: a kind of little 'island', connected to the main building by a drawbridge. The entrance gate is about 15 feet (4·6 m) above the ground, and once the drawbridge was pulled up, it was virtually impossible to get into the fort – or out of it: the fort was also frequently used as a disciplinary institution for misbehaving officials of the WIC.

After the fall of Elmina, the Portuguese still held out for some time in their remaining two forts of Shama and Axim. In 1640 Portugal revolted against its Spanish overlord, Philip IV, and the country regained its independence. This automatically brought Portugal onto the side of the Dutch, in the enemy-camp against the Spanish, a situation which had its political advantages in Europe, but which was highly embarrassing to the chartered East and West Indian companies, as they could no longer claim that they were serving the national cause with their attacks on the Portuguese overseas empire.

In their own interests the Dutch States-General tried to delay as much as possible the ratification of the peace treaty. Although the WIC officials at Elmina were aware of the latest developments in Europe, they felt justified in capturing the Portuguese fort at Shama, as they had not yet received a copy of the ratified treaty. A second expedition, against Axim, was called off as the season was unfavourable: during the rainy season the Guinea current[6] is very strong, and the fleet of merchant ships sent against Axim took more than two weeks to travel the relatively short distance to Takoradi. But by the time that Admiral Jol ('Peg-Leg'), returning from his conquest of Angola and São Tome, attacked Fort St Anthony at Axim, copies of the treaty had definitely been received on the Gold Coast, and the outraged Portuguese fought furiously against their new supposed 'ally'. But the Dutch put some cannon on the little islands off-shore and used them to bombard the fort.

When the fort eventually fell into Dutch hands, it was a ruin. They restored it without changing the general shape much, but later they created a courtyard of a rather irregular, trapezoidal form, by erecting a new building to the north side of the fort, which at some time was even connected to the old building by a kind of wooden fly-over, two storeys high above the ground. The new building was surmounted by two towers. To the east and west side of the old building two rather charming structures were added, providing balconies and arch-ways. Like most forts, Axim fort also acquired in the eighteenth century spacious outworks to the north and west. The western workyard is well preserved.

At the time that the Dutch captured it Fort St Sebastian was hardly more than a ruin, and the tiny Portuguese garrison surrendered without even attempting to resist. Afterwards the Dutch carried out some minor repairs, but it remained a trade post of little importance which the Dutch allowed to be in a poor state of defence. In 1664 the English had little trouble in capturing it from the Dutch (see below, p. 33). But after their recovery of the fort, the Dutch reconstructed it and gave it its present form. The ground plan of the central buildings is probably the same as that of the Portuguese fort, with two round bastions and two pointed ones diagonally opposed (similar to the original plan of Elmina Castle), but the Dutch turned the round SW bastion into a tower and added one storey to the central buildings. They also surrounded the whole building with a wall like Coenraadsburg.

The hillock on which the fort is built consists of soft

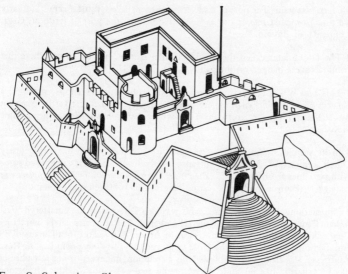

Fort St Sebastian, Shama

laterite stone which is easily washed away by the rains. In the records there are frequent complaints about the sagging or collapsing of the fort's walls as a result of this. Later a solution was found to this problem by building elaborate buttresses all around the fort, from the bottom of the hillock upwards. The tallest of these buttresses was made into the handsome long flight of semi-circular steps leading to the sea-side entrance of the fort, which became its most characteristic feature.

If Shama remained of little importance for the gold trade, it did have a certain fame for its canoe trade: a little upstream from the mouth of the Prah river is an island where great numbers of seaworthy canoes were made out of enormous tree-trunks which were floated down the river. These canoes were not only used by the Africans, but also by European captains who put them on board their vessels in order to use them along other parts of the African coast, in particular the Slave Coast, where these essential means of communication between ship and shore were lacking.

1 Several towns on the Coast have developed as ports of trade of states which had their capitals or main towns elsewhere; the capital of the ancient Accra state for instance, 'Great Accra', and its principal market, Abese, were in the area of

modern Nsawam. The port of trade was therefore called 'Little Accra'. Similarly we find Komenda referred to as 'Little Komenda', the port of trade of 'Great Komenda' or Eguafo.

2 The Dutch later called this bastion *Galgen Battery*, because it was there that criminals were hanged on the gallows.

3 This area was used as a big service yard, with carpentry shops, smithies, a bakery, pigsties, chicken-runs, etc. It was called *Katteplaets* (cat yard) because it was also used for the rearing of civet cats whose secretion was used in the perfume industry.

4 In its simple ornamentation this structure is typical of seventeenth-century Dutch architecture. Above the entrance, on the inside, is a black engraved stone with two lines from psalm 132: *Zion is des Heeren ruste / Dit is Syn woonplaetse in eeuwigheyt* (Zion is the Lord's resting place / This is His eternal habitation).

5 Translation: '. . . from Veere, who was also Director of the Chartered West Indian Company on behalf of the Chamber of Zealand, and lately Director-General on the North and South Coasts of Africa. Arrived on 16th January 1758 and died on 12th March of the same year, aged 41 years'. A poem by one Rev. Andriesse, also from Veere, follows this inscription, but apart from a few phrases like '. . . hardly had he landed here, ere he died . . .' and '. . . this tombstone honours his chilled bones', the inscription is too much obliterated to make sense to the reader. Documents show that this tombstone must have been dedicated to Mr L. J. Van Tets, who indeed died at Elmina on 12th March, 1758. In 1960 chips of a number of other tombstones were found just outside the castle, near the beach. One of them is fairly well preserved and has been displayed near the main entrance gate. It is dedicated to: 'The Memory of the Honourable Sir Nicholas M. Van der Noot de Gietere, in his life-time Director-General of the North and South Coasts of Africa. Died 4th October, 1755', i.e. he was the last-but-one predecessor of the above-mentioned Mr Van Tets.

6 This current along the Guinea Coast, together with the prevailing winds in the same (eastern) direction, decided the general movement of ships. Nearly all ships visited the 'Upper Coast' or western part first, then sailed 'down' to the 'Lower Coast'. Only canoes and small craft ('yachts') were occasionally sent 'upwards': e.g. from Elmina to supply Axim, or from the Slave Coast to Accra.

20

3 Years of confusion and fierce competition: English, Swedish and Danish penetration

English sailors such as Hawkins, Lok and Towrson had visited the Guinea Coast long before the first Dutchmen arrived, but the English Guinea trade was less well organised. In 1618 the 'Governor and Company of Adventurers of London Trading to Guynney and Binney' had been founded, but their achievements were less impressive than their name. Captains sailing for this company of 'Guynney and Binney' did bring home some useful commodities such as dye-wood, but little gold.

In 1631 the company's financial status improved, but perhaps its greatest asset was one Arent Groote, a disgruntled former employee of the Dutch West India Company on the Coast, who decided in that year to put his experience and his influence, in particular among the Fanti, to the service of the English. Although the Dutch had signed an agreement with 'Ambro Braffo' of 'Fantyn' in 1624, giving them the exclusive rights to trade in his 'state' (it is still a matter of discussion whether at that time there really existed anything like a Fanti state), Groote, whom the Braffo may well have remembered, had little difficulty in persuading that chief to sign a similar agreement for the English; it is quite possible that the Braffo acted entirely in good faith, not realising that this stranger whose language he could not understand[1] had changed masters.

A site on a hill near Kormantin was allocated to the company to build a fort. Initially the English built a rather small fortified lodge, which they gradually enlarged. But in 1640 the lodge was destroyed by fire – the English accused the Dutch of having sent saboteurs, and in spite of the latter's vehement denial this may very well have been true –

21

and afterwards a really strong fort was built. It had two round and two square bastions, and on one side it had a 'house' three storeys high. The thick walls between the bastions, and three of the bastions themselves, were filled

Fort Amsterdam, Kormantin

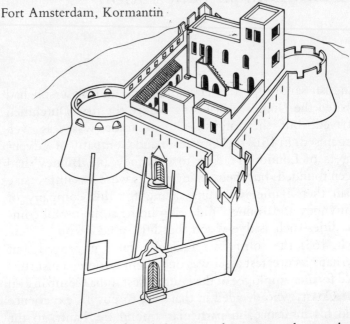

with earth; but the fourth bastion, the one on the south-west, which has now disappeared, was hollow and had a grated ventilation hole in the roof (or platform). Here the English kept the slaves they bought. It was probably the first slave-prison built on the coast; the Portuguese and the Dutch bought their slaves elsewhere in Africa,[2] and still in 1646 a captain arriving at Elmina with forty slaves from 'Ardra' was requested not to disembark them before a number of 'slave-huysjens' or slave barraccoons had been built for them; apparently no room could be found in the vast castle to lodge such a relatively small number of slaves. But the English relied from the onset much more heavily on the Gold Coast for the supply of labour to the West Indian planters. Especially after the conquest of Jamaica in 1655, their needs grew considerably. It is significant that the British West Indian planters, even after the English had lost the fort at Kormantin to the Dutch, continued to refer to slaves from the Gold Coast as 'Cormantins' or 'Coromantese'.

A more serious blow to the supposed Dutch 'monopoly' on the Coast was given by Henry Caerlof; in 1648 he had ended a long and brilliant career in the highest ranks of the hierarchy of the Dutch West India Company on the Coast as Fiscal. But after his return to Europe he met in Amsterdam the son of Louis de Geer, the then famous 'iron-king' of Sweden. The De Geer family, originally exiles from Liège in Belgium (then the Spanish Netherlands), had gone into exile from the Republic of the United Provinces during the civil strife of the second decade of the seventeenth century, and was therefore far from sympathetic towards the West India Company. Caerlof, a Pole by birth, could not be expected to have strong patriotic feelings towards the Republic either, and he readily agreed to return to Africa in the service of a newly created Swedish Africa Company. Later Caerlof admitted to a notary in Amsterdam that this company was entirely financed by Dutch businessmen, and that only the flags and the names of the ships sailing for this company were Swedish.

Caerlof was in an excellent position to set up a whole series of trade-posts all along the coast for his new employers; during his long career in the service of the Dutch West Indian Company he had established friendly relations with a large number of coastal chiefs. Moreover, there was growing discontent among these chiefs with the high-handed way in which the Dutch, who had posed as their 'liberators from the Portuguese yoke', were now making impositions on them. The ease with which the English were extending their influence in the Fanti area also showed clearly that in reality the chiefs there attached little importance to the letter of the contracts of exclusive trading-rights they had signed with the West India Company.

In 1650, for instance, one Crispe had got permission from the King of Fetu to build a fort on the 'Cabo Corço' (Portuguese, meaning 'Short Cape', later corrupted in English to 'Cape Coast') and he 'bought' the land for £64 in goods

23

'whereupon the people gave several great shouts, throwing dust up in the air and proclaimed that this was Crispe's land'. But in the same year Caerlof got permission from the same king to build a lodge on the same land for the Swedish company, and at once established it. A little to the east he took possession of a lodge at Anomabu, which the Dutch had abandoned shortly before on account of the frequent protests and impediments put in their way by the English.

Caerlof then turned his attention to the Western Region; the Dutch had resumed the Portuguese system of levying tolls on African trade (mainly in 'Quaqua' cotton cloth and ivory from the west, and palm-oil, salt and canoes from the east) on the supposed borders of the Axim district, greatly to the dismay of the peoples living beyond those 'borders'. He was therefore received with open arms at Butri, east of Cape Three Points, and at Jumore, in Nzima, and the success of the Swedish lodges there seemed assured.

Finally, Caerlof went to Accra, where he could count on a warm reception: as factor at the Dutch lodge of 'Little Accra' (in 1649 transformed into a fort and named after a famous fortress at Bois-le-Duc, 'Crèvecoeur'), he had in 1646 been sent on a mission to 'Oquy' (Akwamu) to settle a dispute between that kingdom and that of Accra, no doubt in favour of the latter. The King of Accra therefore gladly gave him permission to build a new lodge at Osu, a few miles east of Little Accra. Although Caerlof in fact did nothing more than establish a number of non-fortified lodges, he opened up new outlets for the African trade and thus laid the basis of a number of new forts, two of which were even to be raised to the status of 'castle'.

On the whole, the Dutch West India Company assumed a rather passive attitude; perhaps the penetration of the Swedish company into the Central Region was not even unwelcome to them: it weakened the position of their much more dangerous English competitors rather than their own. The Dutch did not want to pick a quarrel with the King of Accra on account of the small lodge at Osu, which could not be expected to pose a threat to the trade of their better situated brand-new fort Crèvecoeur. But in the Western

Region the Dutch were eager to stop the Swedish threat. Aware that gold-producing areas were not far inland from this part of the coast, they wanted to maintain a strict monopoly. In 1653 the Dutch persuaded the people of 'Encasser'[3] to attack Butri and drive out the Swedish Company. These people had been made allies of the Dutch by Caerlof himself, when he had tried with their help to stop the people of Axim from trading clandestinely with the English. The Swedes opened another lodge at Takoradi, but when three years later they returned to Butri they found the Dutch busy building a fort on top of the high hill commanding the little bay. Not finding much co-operation among the local population, the Dutch probably used for the construction of this fort, which they named 'Batenstein', labourers from Egya, a village in the Fanti area with which the West India Company had friendly relations. Some of these Egya people settled in a small village on terraces just below the fort. Later some clashes would occur between this 'Upper' or 'Adja' village and the Ahanta people of Butri itself (see below, Chapter 6). The fort was originally built in the form of low bastions with two 'houses' on top. Bosman described it as a 'tiny, ill-designed fort' which could hardly stand the firing of its own guns, but its position on the high steep hill, no matter how tiresome to climb, more than a hundred wooden steps up, made it virtually unassailable. In fact, its few guns never had to defend it against foreign attack and have only been used to fire salutes.

In 1872 Batenstein was handed over to the British, who, however, never garrisoned it, although at that time it still seems to have been in good repair. Butri never became an important trading-station, but Batenstein was a useful 'service-fort': timber for repairing other forts and ships was easily conveyed along the nearby river of the same name, and ships could undergo minor repairs in the quiet waters of the bay. A few attempts were also made by the Dutch to open sugar, cotton and coffee plantations on the fertile lands behind the fort and along the river. Even in the 1950s a small jetty and a shed were still in use, west of the village, to embark barrels of palm-oil from the nearby Sese oil-mill on ships waiting in the roads.

In the eighteenth century the fort was reconstructed and a new building was erected between the two wings. This gave the fort a peculiar form, as the two useless bastions on the north side were now incorporated in the main building. Indeed, the fort did not need any defence works on that side, as the slope of the hill is there very steep. Life at this little fort, occupied by only a few men, must have been fairly comfortable in comparison with that in the bigger forts and castles: there was plenty of fresh air, the cistern below the courtyard always provided sufficient good drinking water (from the roofs) and fresh fruits and vegetables were available in abundance; one may however add that life must have been a bit dull at that place – in spite of the beautiful view the fort commands – as trade remained minimal there.

The Swedish settlement at Jumore never became a success. The local chief offered a hut as a lodge, but the 'Swedish' (in reality Swiss) commander who was sent in 1654 to occupy the place was drowned while trying to land, possibly as a result of sabotage by an African agent of the Dutch.

. It was ostensibly to settle a dispute between the States of 'Encasser' and Adom, but also probably to counter the threat of Swedish competition, that the West India Company in 1653 decided to send an expedition to the upper reaches of the Ankobra River, in order to get control over an area which was known for its rich gold-mines. The members of this expedition reported on their return that after travelling more than a week up-stream they had reached a place called 'Dubacqua' where people from Axim used to go to barter sea-salt for gold and where they saw hundreds of gold-pits. The local chief had given permission for the construction of a fort, demanding at the same time that it be well armed: he was aware not only of the possible profits he could derive from the trade with Europeans, but also of the danger of being attacked by jealous neighbours.

The following year a fleet of canoes brought the necessary building materials and a few cannon, for what became known as Fort Ruychaver. This little fort, situated further inland than any European outpost till the end of the nineteenth century, seemed for a few years to be quite a successful trading-post, but in 1659 its commander, one Jan De Liefde, alias de Mancke (the cripple), involved himself in a serious dispute with the local chief about a debt, and was besieged by the angry villagers. In his complete isolation from his fellow Europeans on the coast, he eventually saw no other solution than to set fire to the powderhouse; but before doing so he invited a delegation from his enemies to come to the fort for negotiations, and thus had his final revenge when he was blown up together with his enemies and the fort. It was an untimely end to what had seemed a promising venture; Fort Ruychaver was in fact no more than a wooden structure with a tiled roof and windows which served at the same time as loop-holes for its cannon on top of a base made of mud reinforced with wooden poles, about 22 by 43 feet ($6 \cdot 7$ m $\times$ $14 \cdot 4$m). But at the time of the explosion quantities of stones had already been deposited on top of the hill 'Tinseree or Good Hope' in order to transform it into a really durable fort. The fort was at that time occupied by a factor (De Liefde), an assistant, two soldiers and six company slaves. One of the soldiers also died shortly after the explosion, but the others were taken prisoner by the Adom, who later released them on payment of a ransom.

Although various Dutch administrators made in later years sometimes grandiose plans for a comeback to this approachable gold-mining area (one of them even suggesting the construction of a whole network of fortified tradeposts and the use of a kind of armoured canoes on the river), none of these was ever executed. In 1817 the site of Fort Ruychaver was again located by Colonel Starrenburg who had been sent on an exploratory mission along the Ankobra by the first colonial Governor of the 'Dutch Possessions on the Coast of Guinea', Daendels. Starrenburg only found some rooftiles and some 'formless heaps of stones' near 'Adoea' (Awudua), upon which he planted,

27

quite in style, the Dutch flag.[4]

In 1655 Caerlof returned to Europe, leaving a real Swede, one Krusenstjerna, in charge of affairs on the coast; he was to reside in a new fort, then under construction on the Cabo Corço, called 'Carolusburg' (named after Charles X, 1655–60). Louis de Geer had in the meantime died, and soon Caerlof got involved in a serious quarrel with the heirs of his late friend. This brought him into contact with another section of the Amsterdam business world, which dealt with Sweden's traditional enemy, Denmark. The King of Denmark was at that time busily preparing for war against Sweden, and the financiers of Amsterdam, betting on a Danish victory, were willing to give a financial injection to the ailing Danish East and West India Company (founded in 1650 at Gluckstadt). In 1657 Caerlof once more set out for the Guinea Coast, this time under the Danish flag, with the aim of conquering the Swedish trade-posts he had established himself! In fact, this was not difficult at Osu and at Takoradi, but Krusenstjerna in Carolusburg put up a firm resistance.

However, since the war between Denmark and Sweden in Europe was clearly taking a turn in favour of the Swedes, Director-General Valckenburg at Elmina received instructions to help Caerlof drive out the Swedes: the competition of a defeated Denmark was expected to pose a less serious challenge to the West India Company than that of a victorious Sweden. Consequently Carolusburg fell into Danish hands, and Caerlof sailed back to Europe on board the 'Stockholm Slott', a ship of the Swedish company which he had captured off Cabo Corço; Krusenstjerna was also on board as his prisoner, and a considerable quantity of gold belonging to the Swedish company. In gratitude to the Dutch he gave them permission to take over the Swedish lodge at Jumore, far off in the west, with which he had never been able to do anything.

Meanwhile Denmark and Sweden were negotiating for peace, and both were now chasing Caerlof with his costly prize. He managed to escape them, and bring it safely to Antwerp in the Spanish Netherlands, where he settled as a merchant. On his departure from the Gold Coast, Caerlof had left another renegade of the West Indian Company, one Samuel Smit, in charge of the Danish possessions. A belated 'Swedish' attack (by the Dutch De Vos brothers) on Carolusburg was warded off with help from Elmina, but in 1659, when no Danish ships had been sighted for a long time and the Dutch had convinced Smit of the rumour that Denmark had been 'conquered' by Sweden, he decided to rejoin the ranks of the West India Company, handing over all the 'Danish possessions'. The lodge at Takoradi was shortly afterwards transformed into a fort. To the Dey of Fetu[5] Samuel Smit's behaviour was, however, a gross betrayal of his personal friend Caerlof, and he prevented the Dutch from taking possession of 'Carolusburg'. Finally the Dey decided, in 1660, to sell the fort for a considerable quantity of gold to one of the last remaining representatives of the Swedish company, who borrowed the gold from the English at Kormantin. It was only after the death of this Dey, in 1663, that the Dutch managed to occupy Carolusburg, imprisoning De Vos, its 'Swedish' commander, and thus putting an end to the Swedish enterprise on the Gold Coast.

In the meantime, the Danish company was somewhat reorganised, and took on a more truly national character, although the first commander it sent to the coast, Joos Cramer (from Frankfurt), was also an ex-employee of the Dutch West India Company. Cramer wisely did not interfere in the Carolusburg palaver, and instead negotiated with the Dey of Fetu for the cession of 'Mount Manfro' (Amanful), just a few hundred yards east of the Cabo Corço. On top of that hill, from which heavy guns could easily bombard Carolusburg, a small triangular fort, Fredriksborg or Fredriksberg, was built, mainly of swish and stones, with a thatched 'house'. For a short time Fredriksborg remained the headquarters of the Danes on the Guinea Coast, but soon this role was taken over by a bigger establishment at Osu near Accra (also a former Caerlof settlement) where the Danes carried on most of their trade. Fort Fredriksborg, in spite of its advantageous position, remained therefore

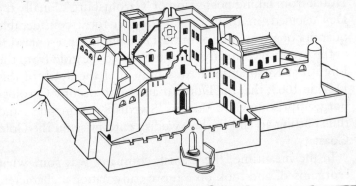

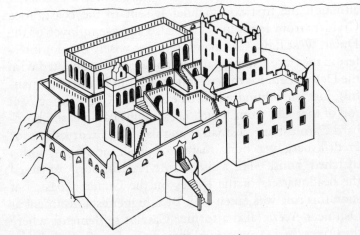

The development of Christiansborg Castle,
17th, 18th and 19th centuries

30

only a minor fort. After 1665, when the English built Cape Coast Castle, the Danes were in no position to challenge them. By 1679 the Danish commander was so much in debt to his English neighbours at Cape Coast, that he had to pawn his own fort to them. In 1685 the Danes eventually sold Fredriksborg to the English. Its greatest asset at that time was 'a fine garden with a summer-house'. In 1699 the English reconstructed the fort, calling it Fort Royal, as an out-fort of Cape Coast Castle, but soon it was abandoned again. At present the vague contours of a triangular building and some old cannon, recovered by a recent Danish excavation, still indicate the site on top of Amanful Hill.

The Danish establishment at Osu was more impressive. The King of Accra, like the Dey of Fetu, we may presume, was indignant at the treachery of Samuel Smit, and told the Dutch to quit Osu. In 1661 Cramer 'bought' a piece of land from King Kangkue of Accra, for the building of a fair-sized stone fort, which was later extended into Christiansborg Castle, the present seat of the Government of Ghana. The present castle is a combination of many extensions of the original one, and has a very irregular form. The castle, especially in its early years, also had an eventful history. In 1679 its commander was killed by mutineers, and their leader, a Greek called Bolten, after a while sold it to the Portuguese former Governor of São Tomé. The Portuguese baptised it 'St Francis Xavier' and occupied it for nearly four years. They built a Roman Catholic chapel in the castle and raised the bastions by three feet (one metre), but it soon became clear that the Portuguese would not be able to stage a successful comeback on the Gold Coast: their merchandise could not compete with that of the English and Dutch. In 1683 the Portuguese sold the castle back to the Danes and quickly evacuated it. It now became the permanent headquarters of the Danes.

Ten years later they lost it to a powerful trader and chief from Akwamu (an inland state which in 1680 had conquered the Accra Kingdom), Assameni, who, with the consent of Bassua, the Akwamuhene, took the fort with a number of his men disguised as merchants. The Danish garrison, already much reduced by death and disease, fled to Fort Crèvecoeur. Assameni occupied the fort for about a year, successfully trading with captains from all nations, receiving them in style (in his early years he had been a cook in the service of the Danes), but in 1694 the Danes bought the castle back from him for the considerable sum of 50 marks of gold. The keys of the castle were not returned, however, and belong to this day to the stool property of Akwamu. With the growing Danish trade, first mainly in gold, later in slaves, the store-rooms and quarters for the garrison were extended, and between the end of the seventeenth and beginning of the nineteenth centuries new bastions, platforms and houses were added, so that the castle ended up nearly four times its original size.

1 For a long time Portuguese remained the *lingua franca* between Europeans and Africans on the Coast.

2 In the sixteenth century the Portuguese had brought slaves from Benin to the Gold Coast in order to sell them for gold; but this trade, as well as that in arms, had been forbidden by royal decree, not on humanitarian grounds, but because it was feared that these slaves and arms would be sold again to the Muslims of the North, and thus strengthen the enemy.

3 It is difficult to identify this people – no state of such name any longer exists, but in Wassa there is still a memory of the 'Ankasa' or 'Nkasa' people 'who do not speak' – *nkasa* in Akan. These people were not allowed to speak of the gold-mines they worked. It is significant that on old maps the area of 'Encasser' is as vague as that of 'Akanny': which can be explained if 'Encassers' stands indeed for 'gold-mines' as 'Akannists' does for 'gold-traders'.

4 Making use of Starrenburg's quite accurate map and description, the author and a colleague from the Archaeology Department of the University of Ghana were in 1969 able to locate the site, approaching from Prestea. In 1975 the Archaeology Department decided to excavate it. Students from Britain and Ghana traced the outline of the fort from quantities of burnt daub where the walls had once been, they found a lot of broken rooftiles and inspected the 'formless heaps of stones' · which Starrenburg had also noted; the latter had certainly not been used for constructional purposes, which confirms the story that the reconstruction of the fort had not yet started at the time of the explosion. The way the rooftiles were scattered over a wide area, and the baked daub of the walls show that the explosion and the ensuing fire must have been quite big. Unfortunately, very few artifacts were found, the ruin of the lodge having been thoroughly ransacked by the local people; but later excavations may reveal more.

5 The title 'Dey' was only used to indicate the chief of Fetu; the origin of the term is uncertain. Most other chiefs were referred to as 'King', or, if less important, as 'Caboceer' or head-man, a term of Portuguese origin.

4 The growth of the English trade and Brandenburg competition

After the Restoration of 1660 the English Guinea trade enjoyed more interest on the part of the Court of St James, and the old Company of Guynney and Binney was replaced by the 'Company of Royal Adventurers of England Trading to Africa', under royal charter. The Duke of York (later James II), in particular, supported the new company. A brisk trade was now carried on at Kormantin, and new English lodges were established at Anashan (modern Biriwa), Winneba and Accra. The English tried to prevent the Dutch from re-settling on the Cabo Corço by blockading that part of the coast, and in retaliation the Dutch made frequent attacks on English ships. In those days relations between England and Holland were rapidly deteriorating, particularly as a result of Charles II's renewal of the Act of Navigation, a protectionist measure earlier employed by Oliver Cromwell which in 1652 had brought about the First Anglo-Dutch Naval War.

The two nations, now clearly preparing for another armed conflict, at first limited themselves to acts of piracy on each other's ships, officially keeping the peace. In 1664 England, no longer willing to put up with Dutch molestations, sent out two strong fleets against Dutch colonies and settlements in the Americas and Africa. The Dutch were not prepared for an onslaught on such a scale in peacetime. The Dutch in the colony of the New Netherlands on the Hudson River soon had to give up the struggle. Their capital New Amsterdam was taken and named New York after James, Duke of York, Lord High Admiral. In West Africa Admiral Holmes took in quick succession the Dutch forts on the island of Gorée (off Dakar), at Takoradi, Shama

33

and Mori, and the lodges in Sierra Leone and at Anomabu and Egya. The Dey of Fetu did not oppose the English, who with the help of the Danes of Fredriksborg drove the Dutch out of Carolusburg, less than a year after they had bought it.

The Dutch were indeed taken by surprise. But the States-General, once the news of Holmes' exploits had reached the Netherlands, did not allow itself to be dragged into an untimely declaration of war; instead it sent a secret message to Admiral De Ruyter, who at that time was stationed with a big fleet off Gibraltar, to sail immediately to the Guinea Coast, in order to recapture the lost possessions and to take the English headquarters at Kormantin. Another fleet set out for South America, where the Dutch made up for the loss of the New Netherlands (New York) by taking the English plantation colony on the Surinam River (Guyana). De Ruyter's expedition was as unexpected to the English as that of Holmes had been to the Dutch. Without much trouble De Ruyter recovered the fort on Gorée and the lodge in Sierra Leone, but at Takoradi he met with strong resistance, not only from the English but also from the Africans, who were 'great enemies of those of Elmina'. The fort was, however, rather small, and after prolonged bombardment the English had to capitulate. Shortly afterwards 'the sea became black with canoes from Elmina'.

These African auxiliaries wrought a terrible massacre among the people of Takoradi. As that place was no longer considered safe for a Dutch establishment, De Ruyter received orders to demolish the remains of the fort: he wrote with satisfaction that when he blew it up 'it went straight up into the air'. The English had apparently not been able to keep Shama, and by the time De Ruyter passed that fort it was again occupied by a Dutch garrison. But he was advised not to take water at that place, because 'the negroes have not yet been pardoned by Governor Valckenburg'. De Ruyter then stayed for about a month at Elmina, making plans for an attack on the English headquarters at Kormantin and on Carolusburg.

The English had in the meantime greatly extended and

reinforced the latter, and armed it with heavy guns. In fact the Admiral felt rather insecure: he was waiting for reinforcements from Holland, but at the same time an English fleet under the command of Charles II's cousin Prince Rupert was expected. Eventually, when neither of them had arrived, De Ruyter undertook the attack on the fort at Kormantin. After a long and bloody battle this was taken with the help of the African auxiliaries from Sabu and Fanti – even from Kormantin itself – but the latter asked a heavy price for it. Apart from a lump sum the Dutch had to pay, any vessels trading there had henceforward to pay enormous 'ships' gifts' before starting to trade.

The English had already abandoned Anomabu and Mori, probably to reinforce their position in Carolusburg. This fort was now so strong that De Ruyter saw no chance of attacking it with success; moreover, he had received orders to continue his expedition to America and to return home from there. Eventually war was officially declared, and his presence in the European seas, where most of the war was fought, was badly needed. At the Peace of Breda (1668) it was agreed that both parties should keep their conquests.

The events of 1664–65 led to considerable building activity. The English and Dutch had now shown each other that strong fortifications were a necessity. After the fall of Kormantin, the much extended Carolusburg became the English headquarters, known as Cape Coast Castle. The Dutch reconstructed their new acquisition at Kormantin and named it Fort Amsterdam (perhaps to avenge their recent loss of New Amsterdam to the English!), built the new Fort Coenraadsburg to replace the simple fortification on St Jago Hill, gave Fort St Sebastian at Shama much of its present form, reinforced Crèvecoeur at Accra and reconditioned Fort Nassau at Mori. The English, in order to concentrate on the defence of Kormantin, had abandoned the recently captured fortified lodge at Anomabu, and blown it up. Neither the English nor the Dutch dared to re-occupy the abandoned lodges at Egya, Anashan and Mt Cong (later Queen Anne's Point, near Cape Coast). The English, for the time being, mainly occupied themselves with the construction of the new Cape Coast Castle. Soon little could be recognised of the old Carolusburg.

In the late 1660s the star of both the English and the Dutch companies declined, however, because of financial difficulties. In 1672, the 'Year of Disaster' in Dutch history, when the Republic was attacked from three sides, the Company of Royal Adventurers, which has been described as 'an aristocratic treasure-hunt rather than an organised business', was abolished, and the English Guinea trade was put on a much sounder financial basis in the new Royal African Company. The Dutch West India Company, whose charter was due for renewal in 1674, was by that time completely bankrupt. Consequently the company was liquidated, but in the same year a New West India Company was set up, in organisation very similar to the old one, but on a more modest basis.

While the Dutch were simultaneously fighting their Third Naval War against England (1672–74) and a war against France (1672–78), their new company started off with serious financial difficulties; the vigorous British Royal African Company had little difficulty in quickly extending its influence on the Coast. This time the English avoided an armed conflict but instead weakened the position of the Dutch by building a number of forts and lodges near those of the Dutch, such as those at Anomabu (named after Charles II), Accra (named after his brother and heir, James) and Winneba. Their lodges at Anashan and Egya were also reopened. When in 1682 the Dutch built a new fort at Sekondi (Fort Oranje), the English soon opened there a lodge of their own only a few hundred yards away – with the consent of the local chief. Feeling betrayed by the people of Sekondi, the Dutch again built a little fort at nearby Takoradi (Fort Witsen), where they brought all their goods and personnel from Sekondi, telling the people of that town that they would not come back unless they ejected the English. Eventually the people of Sekondi came to Takoradi, requesting that the Dutch return to their town, because the English had very little to offer. As Sekondi was better situated for trade than Takoradi, the Dutch did indeed return there, but the English, who had in the meantime extended their lodge into a fort, were there to stay.

Meanwhile, new competitors were appearing on the western part of the Gold Coast in the form of the Brandenburg Africa Company. In 1682 Benjamin Raule, a member of a great Huguenot corsair family from Dunkirk which had lately settled at Flushing, in Zealand (also an important port of corsairs), founded a new 'interloper company', for the 'Great Elector', Frederick William of Brandenburg. Raule had earlier, during Brandenburg's war with Sweden (1674–78), offered the Elector the services of his corsairs in capturing ships (mainly Dutch ones) bringing military stores to Sweden. He had so much ingratiated himself with the Elector that the latter appointed him his Minister of Marine. When Raule found a number of financiers and ship-owners in Amsterdam willing to co-operate and to organise a new company for the purpose of breaking the West Indian Company's monopoly in West Africa, the Elector happily lent his flag for coverage. With this new *Kurfürstliche Afrikanisch-Brandenburgische Compagnie* his state would also belong to that select club of European nations engaged in the prestigious business of overseas expansion.

The Brandenburg Africa Company concentrated mainly on the Ahanta area, which was believed to be most favourably situated for the gold-trade. One of the first ships of the new company returning to Europe took on board some ambassadors from the Chief of Pokesu, just west of Cape Three Points, near the mouth of the river Nyan. These ambassadors were received with full honours at the electoral court in Berlin, and returned with the next ship. In 1683 the Chief of Pokesu drank 'fetish' (a mixture of brandy and gunpowder) with the first Brandenburg Governor, one Von der Groben. A promontory near the village was ceded to the Brandenburgers, who for their part promised to protect the people of Pokesu (which later became known as 'Prinze Terre' or Princes Town), against attacks by the Dutch, and never to sell their wives and children as slaves.

Shortly afterwards the Brandenburg company began the

37

construction of a major fort, which was called Gross Friedrichsburg, after the Elector. From the outset the Brandenburgers were aware of the risk of attack by the Dutch and
their African allies, and therefore the fort, even while under
construction, was heavily armed. Eventually it had 32
heavy cannon. By 1684 the four bastions, with unusually
thick parapets and linked by wide curtain walls made of
solid masonry, were ready. The enclosure initially looked
'like a farm-yard', but soon some two-storey buildings

Fort Gross Friedrichsburg,
Princes Town

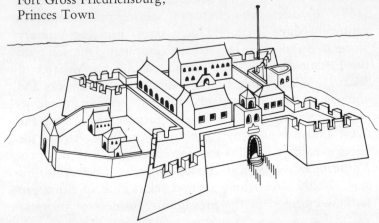

were constructed for the no fewer than 91 Europeans of this
mainly military establishment. The fort, with its monumental gateway (with a big bell-tower) became one of the
most luxurious forts on the coast, and typical of late
seventeenth-century Brandenburg, always out to impress
the world with its new might.

In the following years the Brandenburg company built
Fort Dorothea near Akwida (Accoda) east of Cape Three
Points and Fort Louise at Takrama on Cape Three Points
itself. Fort Dorothea was originally built as a small triangular building. Situated on a promontory and the end of a
peninsula between the mouth of the Suni River and the sea,
it had much natural protection. Shortly after its construction it was taken by the Dutch, but as the Republic did not
want to lose its valuable alliance with Brandenburg against
Louis XIV on account of some petty quarrels in distant

38

Ahanta, the fort was soon given back to the Brandenburg company. Later it was a little extended, probably by the Germans, who turned it into a square building with two bastions pointing landwards. After the Dutch had taken it over – in the early eighteenth century – it fell into decay, but the masonry is so solid that even after more than 250 years much of the little fort is still standing.

Little is known of the fort at Takrama. It was probably not much more than a fortified lodge, and the rocky coast of Cape Three Points must have made it very difficult to approach from the sea. In 1684 the Brandenburg company also started to build a lodge at Takoradi, but before they had finished the Dutch once more occupied Fort Witsen, and the Brandenburgers had to give up all attempts there.

From the military point of view the Brandenburg establishments were impressive, but commercially they could hardly be called an asset. The Elector had clearly over-reached himself in this respect, and had to continue to rely on Dutch 'expertise'. These Dutch merchants, most of them renegades of the West India Company, were on the whole very corrupt, and within ten years the Brandenburg company was on the verge of collapse. So was Gross Friedrichsburg itself in 1693, but in that year it was restored, and an outwork was built as a service-yard. As ships of the Brandenburg company only rarely arrived, the company's officials traded with ships from all nations, and Gross Friedrichsburg was to remain for a long time the most important smuggling station on the Coast. Gradually the fort began to lose its military character, and one of the last additions to the fort, a big round tower against the north-east curtain wall, built in 1708, is typical of this development. Probably built as a kind of buttress to prevent the wall's sagging, it provides a very pleasant and fresh room at the top, but actually renders half of the two north bastions useless.

5 Tensions and turmoils around 1700

In the 1680s the Royal African Company became quite prosperous. It traded considerable quantities of gold, which were minted in London as the famous 'Guineas'. These coins, stamped on one side with the emblem of the Royal African Company, soon had an intrinsic value which exceeded that of the Pound Sterling, and until quite recently (when Britain 'went decimal') the term 'guinea' continued to be used to indicate a 'heavy' pound, worth 21 shillings.

But even more profitable was the slave trade. That trade increased enormously during the second half of the seventeenth century with the rapidly expanding plantation economies of the West Indian islands. The Dutch initially took the lion's share in the slave trade, and even controlled for some time, in the 1680s, the Spanish Asiento. But they relied for their slave supplies mainly on the Slave Coast, the Bight of Biafra and Angola, reserving the Gold Coast, as the Portuguese had done before them, exclusively for the gold trade. The English, however, did not follow the same policy, and soon the slave trade brought much more revenue to the Royal African Company than the gold trade; the English, in their quest for slaves, brought great quantities of firearms to the Gold Coast, and soon the Dutch were obliged to do the same and therefore give up their earlier policy of excluding firearms from the Gold Coast trade.

In the 1680s Cape Coast Castle underwent major changes: the north side was much extended, ending in what is still known as 'Greenhill's Point'. Between this new bastion, which protected the narrow strip of beach east of the castle, the only place where canoes could safely land,

and another new building on the south, facing the sea, a long low platform was built, mounted with many guns. The large, more or less triangular parade which was thus formed covered some large vaults, ventilated with gratings along the sides. These vaults were used as slave prisons and could contain more than a thousand slaves awaiting shipment. Barbot remarked about this arrangement: 'the keeping of slaves thus underground is a good security to the garrison against insurrection', but admitted that the slaves' health was bound to suffer in these appalling dark holes. There were also cisterns under this square but they were not big enough to supply drinking water for everybody and frequently the inhabitants of the castle had to resort to ponds in the garden behind the town.

In 1687, when competition among the English, Dutch, Danes and Brandenburgers was fierce, the French also established trade-posts at Assini (just across the border of the modern Ivory Coast) and at Komenda. Since 1638 the French had made several attempts to establish themselves at the latter place; they had also taken several ambassadors from the Komenda or Eguafo State with them to France, where they were invariably received with full honours (there was a certain romantic aura around these 'Black Princes'), but they had never managed to build a fort or even a simple lodge at Komenda or any other place along the Gold Coast. The Dutch and English had intermittently occupied lodges at Komenda, but in 1687 neither could prevent the Sieur Ducasse, arriving with a strong squadron, from establishing a fairly large trade-post of six houses there. The French established friendly relations with the rich trader and chief John Kabes, who was later punished by the Dutch for his 'betrayal'. But a month after the French trade-post had been finished the Dutch sent a large number of men from Elmina and Eguafo to set fire to it, and Ducasse had to look passively on while it went up in flames.

This episode, however, later led to a civil war within the Eguafo state between a pro-French and a pro-Dutch party. In fact the king felt betrayed by the French, because when making an agreement with them he had explicitly demanded that they build a strong fort, and not a simple trade-post. Before attacking the French establishment the Dutch had made an agreement in which they not only promised to build a fort, but also asked the people of Komenda not to attack the English lodge there. The English, however, did not know this, and left Komenda at the same time as the French. In 1689 the Dutch built a small but strong fort, 'Vredenburgh', on the left bank of the Komenda River, but their position was seriously impaired by the fact that they had offended the most powerful man in Komenda, John Kabes.

Kabes became the central figure in a succession of conflicts known as the Komenda Wars, joining now the English, now the Dutch, and involving a number of neighbouring states, on the coast as well as in the interior. These wars broke out as a result of an incident in which some people employed by the Dutch Company to mine gold in a hill near Komenda were suddenly attacked. This attack, as it appeared later, had been masterminded by John Kabes, who earlier, in an apparent act of reconciliation, had invited them to try their luck in this 'Sika Bergh' (as the Dutch

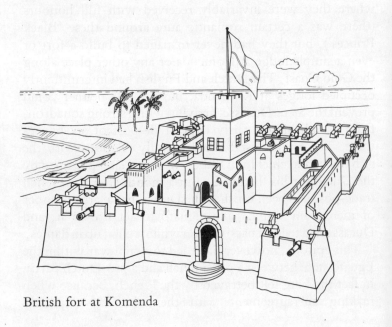

British fort at Komenda

called it) or 'Money Hill' (its English name). This must have been virtually the same site as the one at which the Portuguese had met with disaster seventy years earlier. During these wars several chiefs succeeded one another in the Eguafo state: some were killed in battle, others destooled, one was even murdered in Cape Coast Castle; but all were in the pay of either the Dutch or the English. In 1694 the English, with the support of John Kabes, built a fort within the range of Fort Vredenburgh, on the right bank of the Komenda river. This helped to sharpen the conflict, which lasted beyond the turn of the century.

The ruins of the Dutch and the British forts still stand on the opposite banks of the Komenda river as monuments of the political rivalries within the Eguafo state rather than the commercial importance of the town which was too near to Elmina and Cape Coast to develop as an important port of trade. It is remarkable that the Royal African Company and the West Indian Company were involved in this fierce competition at a time when, at home, the English and the Dutch were more closely linked than ever, acting together under one sovereign, William III of Orange, to thwart the expansionist policies of Louis XIV of France. The division of Komenda town became permanent, and even today the township on the east bank of the river is still known as 'Dutch Komenda' while that on the west bank goes under the name of 'British Komenda'.

Shortly after this episode of the Komenda wars, the Royal African Company sent a most redoubtable figure to the Coast as Agent: Sir Dalby Thomas. Dalby Thomas was almost constantly in conflict with his counterparts in Elmina Castle, and he was determined to divert the trade from Elmina to British stations. If he could not convince all African traders to bring their wares to Cape Coast Castle, he thought he could attract them to British Komenda by offering them the safety of an extra-strong fort.

The new fort the British built at Komenda in 1708 was an extraordinary structure: it consisted of a large square fortification with bastions, built of local rock and with an extra-reinforced curtain wall on the side facing the Dutch

fort, within which was built a much higher building, surmounted by a tower, on exactly the same, but much
reduced, ground-plan. The space between the outer fort
and the central building offered indeed much more safety to
visiting traders or local people than the traditional spurs,
but the tiny inner fort can only have offered very cramped
living conditions. William Smith's 1727 plan of the British
fort at Sekondi, also built within a few hundred yards from

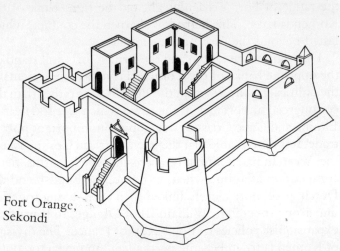

Fort Orange,
Sekondi

a Dutch fort, shows a similar design; there the inner fort and
the outer fort had, however, only two bastions each, and
the inner fort was not placed in the centre. Unfortunately,
only a few traces are left of the British fort at Sekondi.

The turmoils of the Komenda wars, during which great
quantities of firearms were distributed by the English and
the Dutch to their respective allies, and which were
immediately followed by the great wars in the interior from
which Ashanti emerged as the supreme power, had a very
adverse influence on trade, particularly in gold. This may
explain why both the English and the Dutch continued to
cast covetous eyes on Komenda's 'Money Hill'. Although
this hill was first 'ceded' to the Dutch, and then to the
English, and both tried by ingenious ways to extract gold
from its flanks, neither of them ever succeeded in producing
even an ounce of that precious metal.

The traditional ports of trade no longer supplying sufficient quantities of gold, the English and the Dutch began to look for new places where they could tap the flow of gold. Also in order to check the many English captains who traded at 'Gross Friedrichsburg', the Royal African Company decided to build a fort in the Ahanta area. A promontory near Infuma, a village which later became known as 'Dick's Cove' or Dixcove, as it was situated on the shore of a little rocky cove, was chosen as its site. In 1692 construction started, but it progressed slowly, due to lack of co-operation on the part of the local people, divided among themselves: the small community of Infuma consisted of immigrants from two areas and maintained (and in fact still maintains) two chiefs. In 1696 the fort, not yet entirely finished, had to endure a siege by the Ahanta.

Dixcove Fort, which until 1868 was the only English possession in this area, was in fact besieged many times. The trade at this place was far from flourishing, and the gold which the English bought there was often very impure. Bosman, not without gloating, wrote that Dixcove was known as 'the fake mint of the Gold Coast'. In fact, Dixcove Fort in later years fulfilled for the English much the same role as the fort at Butri did for the Dutch: it became a service-fort: it was the only English fort in a densely-wooded area, from which timber for the repair of ships and other forts could be taken. The cove, like Butri Bay, was deep enough for small ships to enter and to undergo repairs.

The Dutch at that time tried to open up another area for their trade: the little state of 'Acron' between Fanti and Agona was apparently willing to allow them to establish a fort at Apam. The Directors of the West India Company were not very happy with the plan of their representative at Elmina to build yet another fort on the Guinea Coast. Returns from that area had been minimal over the last years; but eventually they consented, on condition that it was done at the smallest possible expense. The result, Fort 'Leydsaemheyt', was indeed hardly an impressive building: a small two-storey house flanked by only two bastions. A small spur in front of this building, containing the entrance

Fort Leydsaemsheyt,
Apam

gate, the guard room, some store rooms and the prison, functioned as a kind of courtyard. The 'prison' is so tiny that one wonders if it could contain more than two or three persons. The guard room has now disappeared, and the gate leading from this room to the courtyard has now in fact become the main gate; the plan of the original guard room can however still be recognised in the low wall in front of this new gate, although the original gate was blocked, and the steps leading to the entrance are now made on the side of the original guard room. Later, two fairly sizable service yards were added to the south and west, within which a number of new buildings were erected, like the two-storey wing pointing to the south which contained the 'Orange Hall'; several Dutch forts had such an 'Orange Hall', which served as a kind of reception room, common room or 'palaver hall'. These extensions were not defended by bastions or curtain walls, and were built at a time when the Dutch had come to some sort of common understanding with the surrounding people. But initially the political conditions under which the Dutch constructed their fort at Apam were quite similar to those under which the English were living at that time at Dixcove. The big neighbours of tiny Acron, Agona in the east and Fanti in the west, were allies of the British. The people of Acron wished to see a strong fort to defend them in case of attack, and repeatedly threatened the Dutch with expulsion when they saw how small the fort was to be. Consequently the construction of the tiny building took nearly five years, which made the Dutch decide to call it 'Patience'.

In 1701 the French seemed once more poised to take their share in the Gold Coast trade. They extended their lodge at Assini into the real Fort St Louis – albeit a largely wooden fort – and it was feared that this time they might also build forts farther to the east. In fact, they went to Accra to negotiate for that purpose with the Akwamuhene, but the Dutch Director-General was quick to remind the Akwamuhene of his promise not to allow other nations to build new trade-posts on his territory. The West India Company also feared that the French might attempt to acquire a base at the mouth of the Ankobra River. The Dutch had for some time maintained a stone 'toll-house' at approximately the site where the ticket-office for the Ankobra Ferry now stands, but had eventually abandoned it as the traders refused to pay the tolls. On the pretext of defending the company's interests at the mouth of the Ankobra, a squadron of three ships was sent from Elmina in November 1702, but the ships sailed on and began to bombard Fort St Louis at Assini, some 80 miles to the west. When the French seemed to have given up, the Dutch landed troops, but several boats capsized in the heavy surf and those who managed to reach the shore were massacred there by the 'French negroes'.

Although this expedition ended in disaster for the Dutch, the French soon abandoned their little fort. Their main interest was really in the slave trade: in 1701 Louis XIV pretended that he had 'inherited' the right to supply the Spanish asiento, when his grandson, Philip of Anjou, became the new King of Spain. In fact, the French built in 1702 a large fortified lodge, the Fort Français, at Whydah, which would remain the largest European establishment in that area.

The Dutch did in the end establish a big lodge on top of the Mount Ankobra, overlooking the mouth of the river of the same name. Little is known about it. In 1703 some cannon were hauled up the mountain, and there is in the second edition of Bosman's book an engraving representing a large trade-lodge called 'Elise Carthago'. There is also in the collection of maps and plans of the Archives at The Hague a plan for the building of 'the fort at Ankoper'. Possibly this was the plan for the new fort the company wanted to build in 1708 as part of a major scheme for the exploitation of the Ankobra's gold riches. In fact, a number of guns were hauled on top of the hill, and for some time there was a prosperous trade, but before the lodge could be transformed into a fort trade collapsed as a result of wars, and in 1711 the lodge was abandoned. The following year it was burnt down by John Conny.

The victory of Osei Tutu, King of Ashanti, over his former overlord, Ntim Gyakiri of Denkyira, in 1701, did not remain unnoticed on the coast. In that same year the members of the council at Elmina Castle decided to enter upon 'a venture never undertaken before': to send a fully-fledged ambassador on behalf of the company to the court of 'the Great Zaay of Assiantyn' at Kumasi. They chose as their deputy David Van Nyendael, an adventurous man who had earlier shown his diplomatic capabilities in a mission to the Oba of Benin. Van Nyendael, who was an orphan and therefore probably not afraid of loneliness, stayed in Kumasi for more than a year. It is most unfortunate that he was seriously ill when he returned to Elmina, where he died a few days after his arrival, without having submitted the report he was instructed to make about his long residence in the Ashanti capital. The English did not stay behind, and soon sent an ambassador of their own to Kumasi. They, like the Dutch, hoped that this diplomatic activity would lead to a revival of the gold trade, as Ashanti was known to be rich in gold. After some time the first Ashanti traders came indeed to the coast, bringing with them quantities of gold, but 'all the old traders seem to have died', the Dutch noted, 'and the young ones don't know how to go about it'.

The offer of slaves, on the other hand, continued to increase on the coast, and so did the demand for fire arms and ammunition. Particularly the Directors of the WIC in Amsterdam continued to express their dissatisfaction about the returns from the Gold Coast, though Director-General De la Palma tried to convince his superiors in Amsterdam, in 1703, that they should regard the slave trade as 'the true cornerstone of Your Honours' interest . . . the only thing which can make the Noble Company happy', writing at the same time that he needed more guns and powder. But in reality the Dutch had then lost access to the major slave markets in America and the West Indies. Moreover, one of the Agents of the Royal African Company at Cape Coast rightly remarked in 1706 'by custom the Negroes bring their slaves to the English and their gold to the Dutch'.

A few years later the Dutch realised that the gold-trade was in fact still the real cornerstone of their company's interest, but it was too late: the supply of gold from the interior had by then been reduced to a fraction of what it had been in the 'good old days' of the previous century.

In 1704 the Dutch made a last attempt to open a new outlet for the gold-trade. Akim, situated north of Agona, was then considered the most important producer of gold. In that year they asked the Queen of Agona for permission to build a fort at Senya Beraku, where they had already had a lodge in the 1660s, but which they had abandoned when the English built a fort at nearby Winnebah. The Queen agreed, but at the same time gave permission to the English to build a lodge at neighbouring Shido. After some altercations the English abandoned the lodge, but, contrary to their express agreement with the Dutch not to build any new forts or factories or to re-open abandoned ones, they re-occupied at the same time their abandoned fort at Sekondi, whereupon the Dutch built a little triangular fort at Senya Beraku. It was the last fort they would build on the Gold Coast proper, and when it was ready, less than a year afterwards, they called it aptly 'De Goede Hoop' (Good Hope). Their hope was largely in vain: the gold-trade at Senya Beraku never became very prosperous. But in later years numerous slaves were sold at the fort, and by 1715 it had become much too small. The fort was then doubled in

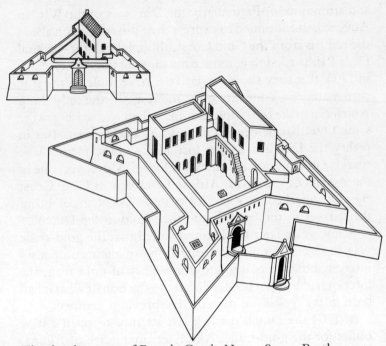

The development of Fort de Goede Hoop, Senya Beraku

size, by making it square and breaking away the diagonal wall (which was probably built of swish). A fairly large slave-prison was made in the south-west bastion. In the second half of the eighteenth century, the fort was surrounded by an outer wall, of which only fragments are at present visible. The fort was recently restored and will soon fulfil its new function of resthouse.

Officials of the WIC at Elmina continued to complain that 'the Gold Coast had changed into a virtual Slave Coast', but it cannot be denied that, particularly in the Western Region, the gold-trade did continue. Gold-traders from Ashanti and Denkyira regularly came to Fort St Anthony at Axim. But many went also to the Prussian (i.e. formerly Brandenburg) forts. One of the most successful African traders at Pokesu was John Conny, the 'broker' of the Prussian company, who wielded much political power. He established links with states of the interior, in order to assure himself of a regular supply of gold. Soon he was referred to as 'the King of Prinze Terre'.

John Conny was a thorn in the flesh of the Dutch, whose trade at Axim, Butri and Sekondi began to decline as a result of his activities. When Conny's men in 1712 attacked Dixcove, the English and Dutch for once co-operated and managed with the help of the Prussian 'General' to settle the palavers between Conny and his neighbours. It was only a temporary solution. In 1714 Conny involved himself again in the affairs of a neighbouring town: at that time there was a quarrel between the 'Adjas' and the 'Antas' of Butri. It was a quarrel of very local character: the 'Adjas', or 'Red Earth People', lived in a few huts on the (red laterite) slope of the hill on which stands Fort Batenstein, and were probably the descendants of the people the Dutch had brought there in the 1650s from Adja or Egya in the Central Region in order to help in the construction of the fort. They were always regarded as aliens by the 'Antas' or 'White Earth People' of Butri village, built on the white sandy beach. When the 'Adjas' killed one Obim, an elder of Butri and a personal friend of John Conny, the latter decided to take revenge on the Adjas and their protectors, the Dutch. Soon this quarrel took on much wider implications, involving powerful states of the interior, such as Wassa and Twifo. In fact, an Ashanti invasion was threatening by the time that the friends of the late Obim killed the leader of the Adjas. Having evacuated the latter from Butri, the Dutch managed however to restore the peace, after lengthy negotiations and the imposition of heavy fines.

On the departure of the last Prussian 'General', in 1716, the affairs of 'Gross Friedrichsburg' were in fact left in the hands of John Conny. In the following year the Prussians decided to sell their African possessions to the Dutch, but Conny was not officially informed about this. Naturally, he refused to budge from what he now considered his fort, and continued to do a brisk trade there with captains from all nations, offering gold and slaves at prices about twenty per cent lower than those at the other forts and castles. In 1718 the Dutch lost patience, and decided to use force to get John Conny out of his stronghold. They sent three ships full of armed men, but the expedition turned out a dismal failure; their bombardment of Pokesu remained without effect and their landing force was ambushed and withdrew after a loss of more than thirty men. On the same day John Conny offered to let a French captain hoist the French flag on his fort, an offer which the captain politely declined on diplomatic considerations. In 1722 the Dutch tried to negotiate with Conny, going to the extent of giving him the right to name himself a (Dutch) commander to the fort and to receive a considerable stipend, but Conny would not budge.

Eventually, in 1724, a second attack was launched on Gross Friedrichsburg, and this time the Dutch succeeded. The fort had in the meantime lost much of its former strength and splendour; Conny had taken many stones from the building in order to build a big house for himself and a wall between the fort and his town. Fort Hollandia, as the Dutch called it afterwards, remained a trading-station of minor importance which was maintained at minimal cost. Commercially it often ranked lower than the much smaller fort at Akwida which was better situated for trade.

6 The last forts of the eighteenth century

During the eighteenth century few new forts were built; the main interest of the Europeans was now in the slave-trade, and, although Gold Coast slaves were much in demand, a place like Whydah, after 1727 Dahomey's port of trade, exported by the middle of the century more slaves alone than all the trading stations on the Gold Coast together. The protectionist ideas of seventeenth-century mercantilism also began gradually to give way to the more liberal ideas of the eighteenth century. The monopolistic approach of the chartered companies no longer proved successful, and the English recognised this earlier than the Dutch. In 1698 the Royal African Company opened up its monopoly area to captains not in its employment on condition that they paid a 'recognition' of ten per cent to the company. These 'Ten Percenters' soon became much more numerous than the company's own ships, and were a headache not only to the Dutch but also to the Royal African Company itself. In 1712 the 'Ten Percent Act' was abolished, and the Guinea trade was open to everybody in England. In 1730 the West India Company opened its monopoly area to free traders on condition that they paid recognition-dues (which in fact they rarely did) – with the exception of the Gold Coast. Four years later, when the old and tired company had entered its fifth charter period, this exception was also dropped.

The British 'Ten Percenters' concentrated in particular on Anomabu, where they bought vast numbers of slaves. As no. official records exist of the activities of these free traders, it is difficult to say how many slaves they bought there; but it seems that the Royal African Company had virtually lost control over this 'Ten Percenters' den', and probably in order to keep at least a stake in the trade of the Fanti area the English built in the 1720s a relatively small fort at Tantumquery (Otuam), a place where about twenty years earlier they had already brought building materials for

British fort at Tantumquery
in the late 19th century

a lodge or a fort, but had been prevented from erecting it by the Dutch of nearby Apam. The fort was later extended with a fairly large triangular spur serving as a service-yard and refuge for the townspeople in time of war. The fort had a regular square shape, and seems to have had a close resemblance to that of Winneba. It was occupied for about a century, but now only some fragmentary ruins remain of it.

Up to the early eighteenth century the coastline east of Accra was considered of little commercial importance, and no European nation had thought it worthwhile to establish trade-posts there. Captains of various nationalities carried on most of their trade in this area at a place known as 'Lay' (or 'Allampo'), which must correspond to modern Lekpongonu. In the late seventeenth century the kingdom of Akwamu began to expand and by 1680 it had Accra under control. Two decades later it commanded the whole coastline eastwards up to Whydah. As Akwamu thus became the only major state of the interior with direct access to the sea, the Europeans began to be more interested in this part of the

'Lower Coast'. The Dutch, who around 1700 were on good terms with the Akwamuhene (who had undergone a successful operation at the hands of the surgeon at Fort Crèvecoeur), got permission to build a lodge at Kpone. The lodge was only intermittently occupied, but a few cannon still lying in the streets of that village remind us that the lodge must have been fortified. Similarly, Dutch documents of the early eighteenth century mention a few times a 'fort' at Tema, but no traces of this fort are known to subsist. The English too, intermittently occupied factories at Prampram and 'Allampo'.

In the 1730s the Akwamu empire collapsed. After a rebellion of the people of Accra and the 'mountain-negroes' of Akwapim it was defeated by Akim. The Danes, who had not been on very good terms with the Akwamu, then profited from the new situation by establishing some trade-posts east of Accra, at Teshi, Ningo, Tubreku near Ada, and Keta. The Dutch, however, tried to prevent the Danes from building more forts, and in 1734–36 there were several clashes when the Danes tried to build their Fort Fredensborg at (Old) Ningo. At that time the Dutch themselves were extending the lodge they had had for some time at Keta into a real fort, called 'Singelenburgh'.

This fort was hardly completed when Agaja, the King of Dahomey, marched in 1737 towards the Volta river, in pursuit of his renegade general, Ashangmo. Ashangmo was one of the leaders of the Ga who in the late seventeenth century had settled at Glidji, in the Popo area (Togo), and who had become famous mercenaries. The year 1737 was one of confusion for Dahomey, and several commanders of its army, among them Ashangmo, mutinied. As the Dutch were known to be good friends of the chiefs of Popo, Agaja suspected that Ashangmo was hiding in or near Fort Singelenburgh. Although the Dutch quite truthfully told the Dahomeans that they knew nothing about Ashangmo's whereabouts, the army of Agaja set up camp under the walls of the fort. Soon they began to forage in the surrounding area and to slaughter cows; they sent deputies to From, the commander of the fort, demanding presents for their king. From sent some presents, but was told that they were not good enough. New presents were sent, but the king became more and more demanding. During the night the Dahomeans began to dig the sand away from under the fort, whose walls soon began to crack. The following day Agaja let it be known that he wanted to talk to From personally, and although his subordinates tried to convince him not to go, From went to the Dahomean camp. Soon it became clear that he was being held prisoner there, and the rest of the garrison saw no other solution than to surrender.

The Dahomeans set off towards their country with their Dutch prisoners, but the latter had told one of their remaining African servants to set fire to the powder house as soon as the Dahomeans entered the building to loot it. Indeed, the prisoners had not gone more than a few hundred yards with an advance party of the Dahomeans when a loud bang told them that their last instructions had been followed. At Aflao one of the Dutchmen managed to escape and he told relatives of Ashangmo what had happened. Soon Ashangmo came out of hiding, and inflicted a terrible defeat on Agaja near Little Popo. The prisoners were released, but From had already been killed. Relations between the Dutch and Agaja were already strained for other reasons, and at that time they lost their last foothold in Dahomey.

When they returned to Keta, they found that the Danes had already settled there, and by 1741 the Danes had so far overcome Dutch intrigues at Ningo that they had been able to build a large fort in peace. This new fort, called 'Fredensborg', was quite well built and armed, but very soon it had to stand the test of its strength.

In 1742 Akim was defeated by Ashanti, and Ashanti troops in that year attacked Ningo. The townspeople sought refuge in the fort, but it was too small to protect all of them, and many of those who had to stay outside were massacred. Fort Fredensborg remained a fairly important trading-station, especially for slave-traders, but after the abolition it soon decayed, and by 1835 only one man was stationed in the fort 'to maintain the flag'. When the British bought it in 1850 with the other Danish possessions, it was already in ruins. At present only a few fragments of its walls can be seen.

In 1754 the Danish West India and Guinea Company was abolished and the Crown took over its possessions. The 'General Trading Company' which took care of the Guinea trade on its behalf was not much of a success either. In 1757 the Danes at Christiansborg were very embarrassed to see the people of Teshi put themselves under Dutch protection. The Danish trade seemed to revive when in 1765 a rich Copenhagen merchant, Bargum, organised the Guinea trade under royal charter, but within ten years this company was also bankrupt. In 1775 the Dutch sent men to the area at the mouth of the Volta to establish a new lodge there, to which the Danes did not object initially, but soon it became clear that they were actually aiming at driving the Danes out of their lodge at Tubreku near Ada. The Danes at Christiansborg then incited the people of Osu to attack Dutch Accra, and a local war ensued which was to last until 1778. The people of Dutch Accra struck back hard, but the Danes were able to ward them off successfully, thanks to a new redoubt, Prøvesten, which they had just built a short distance north-west of the castle.

Shortly afterwards, during the Fourth Anglo-Dutch Naval War (see below, p. 63), Fort Crèvecoeur was however nearly destroyed, and the Dutch, not only from that fort, but also from Kpone, Tema and Teshi, were compelled to take refuge with the Danes at Christiansborg. The Royal Baltic and Guinea Company, founded in 1779, profited considerably from the American War of Independence, and once more the Danish Guinea trade, in particular the slave-trade, revived. The Dutch did not re-occupy their trade-posts east of Accra, and the Danes had the whole coast to themselves as far as Popo (with the exception of Prampram, where the British kept a small trade-post). The Danes had a fortified lodge on an island in the Volta near Ada, which, as well as their lodge at Keta, was frequently exposed to attacks by the people of Awuna.

In 1783 Governor Kiøge decided to put an end to this. A

large-scale military expedition was sent, which defeated the Awuna in the muddy marshlands of the Volta delta, and in 1783–84 two new forts were built, mainly to protect Danish trade against African attack: Fort Kongensten at Ada and Fort Prindsensten at Keta. These were fairly large and strong forts – stones for the fort at Keta were specially conveyed from Accra – of a regular square shape, with four bastions, but they were military rather than trade forts.

In 1787 the Danes built the last of the Gold Coast forts, Fort Augustaborg at Teshi. However, the Danish Guinea trade soon declined again, especially when in 1792 Denmark abolished the slave-trade – the first European nation to do so – and when in 1803 the last Danish slave ship left the Guinea Coast, the last profits from that coast went too for the Danes.

Of Fort Kongenstein at Ada, nothing but a few cannon remain to be seen today. Of Augustaborg, at Teshi, the observant visitor can still recognise a few bits of wall and arches between modern houses. Fort Prindsensten, at Keta, on the other hand, has been fairly well preserved, although in recent days it has undergone several alterations; it serves at present as a prison.

After 1740 the Royal African Company quickly declined; the tiny Fort Vernon, built at Prampram in 1742, is typical of the impoverished state of the company. It was built with the cheapest materials: rough stones and swish, and had only one bastion, significantly pointing to the north-east, that is the landside. Attached to it was a palisade, which could be regarded as a kind of primitive 'spur', but it was also described as a mere 'sheep pen'. In the 1760s another bastion, diagonally opposite the first one, seems to have been built, but it soon collapsed. The ruin of the fort has been transformed into a resthouse, but very little can now be recognised of the original structure.

In 1750 the Royal African Company was replaced by the Committee of Merchants Trading to Africa, which took over the forts in 1752. Under the Committee of Merchants there was some renewed British building activity. In 1751 the French, now frequent visitors to the coast, actually managed to build a small fort at Anomabu, where the old Fort Charles had been abandoned by the British in 1731; they had even gone to the extent of demolishing it, for fear that others might take it over. The people of Anomabu were powerful traders, but the British accused them of profiteering, 'artfully raising the price of Gold, Negroes and Ivory exorbitantly'. Seeing that the French, their archrivals in overseas expansion, were settling at Anomabu they regretted having demolished their old (triangular) fort, and did their best to draw their former 'broker', John Currantee (Koranteng) again to their side with generous gifts and promises. So did the French, and Koranteng profited greatly from this competition for his favours: eventually he had sons studying in both London and Paris at his patrons' expense. In the end, however, the British proved to be the stronger, and in 1753 the French were expelled from Anomabu. In that year British Parliament voted considerable funds for the construction of a new fort; by 1757 it was finished. Built almost entirely with local materials, such as millions of locally burnt bricks, it became one of the handsomest and best built of the Coast. It is now known as Fort William, but that name was probably given to it by its nineteenth-century commander Brodie Cruickshank, who added one storey to the main building, in the days of King William IV.

Most of the other British forts were not as well built as the fort at Anomabu. Their buildings were often made of swish and natural stone which were protected against rain by lime-wash. If they used bricks, they generally produced them locally; although cheaper than imported ones, they were less durable. There were frequent complaints about collapsing walls, sometimes whole bastions, at Cape Coast Castle, which was also notorious for its leaking roofs. After 1760, however, the castle was entirely reconstructed, in stages.

In 1762 a vast new spur, ending in a big round tower, was added to the west side. Along the sides of the spur a series of rooms was built; the spur can in fact be said to have become an integral part of the castle. In 1773 the last remnants of the

59

old Carolusburg were demolished, and a high new building was erected all along the north curtain. The old big bastion at the eastern extremity of the castle, known as 'Greenhill Point' was also replaced by a new structure consisting of two smaller bastions between which a new gate was constructed, the 'Sea Gate', which gives access to the beach on that side of the castle. Ramps from the beach made it possible to roll heavy casks into the castle as soon as they were landed.

Another major addition of those years is the double bastion on the south side of the building, known as 'Grossle's Bastion'. These very well constructed bastions could carry heavy cannon, and made the old low round tower on that side redundant as a defence-work. This allowed Governor Dalzel in the 1790s to put two storeys on top of it, thus transforming it into an integral wing of the central building. The spacious round rooms in the Dalzel Tower were the best in the castle and became governors' apartments. Deep down, below it, inside the new Grossle's Bastions, were the worst rooms of the castle: the slave dungeons. These musty rooms were originally not as dark as they are now, as they had fairly large openings near their ceilings towards the inside of the castle, which are now blocked by later additions. At the time they were considered an improvement on the old dungeons below the parade which had only ventilation through small openings in the roofs, which, like those of the holds of slave ships, had to be closed when it rained, leaving the slaves in airless darkness. These old dungeons were later used as cisterns, while after the abolition of the slave trade the new ones were used as storerooms. The present ramp leading into these dungeons was probably constructed in the nineteenth century in order to facilitate the storage of heavy goods.

In the late eighteenth century some of the new architectural concepts applied in Cape Coast Castle were also used, on a much smaller scale, in the reconstruction of Dixcove fort. Dixcove remained a thorn in the flesh of the Dutch, whose full control of the political affairs of the Ahanta area was disturbed by this British enclave. They often engaged

Dixcove Fort

in long drawn out quarrels with the British about minor issues, such as the right of cutting timber in the forests near Dixcove and instigated their allies to attack the fort. The old spur, built in the days of John Conny, was no longer sufficient, and a new one, containing rooms, like the one at Cape Coast, was constructed, allowing the positioning of a number of heavy guns on the roofs of this new wing. The point of the spur was truncated and provided with a new main gate, flanked by two bastions in much the same way as the 'Sea Gate' of Cape Coast Castle.

In the eighteenth century both the English and the Dutch extended their forts with spurs and outworks, not only to serve as service-yards, but also to keep slaves, when there were too many for the dungeons. More and more frequently, too, they served in time of war as a place of refuge for Africans living near the fort, especially women and children.

The Committee of Merchants built one new fort: that of Apollonia at Beyin. After the Dutch had left Jumore in the 1670s, no European nation had tried to settle on the long sandy beach west of the mouth of the Ankobra, apart from the French with their short-lived fort at Assini. Yet, much gold from the western gold-bearing area was brought to this part of the coast, where captains of all nationalities bartered for it eagerly. As soon as the people of the coastal villages had some gold – or slaves – for sale they would make smoke or other signs to attract passing ships. In the

Fort Apollonia at Beyin

1750s the Nzima chief Amenihyia tried to prevent African traders from going with their goods and slaves to Axim. The Dutch in turn tried to invade the Nzima country (Apollonia) but were beaten off as soon as they crossed the Ankobra. The Dutch did not give up, however, and intermittent warfare continued for a long time. The British began to interfere, and eventually Amenihyia gave them permission to build a fort at Beyin, on slightly elevated solid ground known as Cape Apollonia. In 1766 the English began to blast rocks on a site six miles (10 km) to the west to provide building materials, and two years later they started to build a fort of a quite original new design: one of its four bastions, the one closest to the sea, was made much stronger and bigger than the others, which gave the fort its peculiar shape. Fort Apollonia was also the only English fort which right from the outset was sturdily built; although it remained a fort of only minor importance and was often abandoned for long periods, its ruins were a few years ago still in such good shape that it was not difficult to restore the fort, which is at present in use as a resthouse.

In the second half of the eighteenth century the colonial rivalry between England and France rose to a peak, and its effects were also felt on the Gold Coast. In 1757, during the Seven Years' War, a French naval squadron bombarded Cape Coast Castle, which was badly damaged. The near success of this French attack must also have been a major consideration for reconstructing the castle with more durable materials, and to build better defences on the sea side, like Grossle's bastion.

In 1779 the French attacked British Sekondi, clearly with the connivance of the Dutch there, for they did not make the least attempt to come to the aid of their British neighbours, whose fort the French razed to the ground. Although officially neutral during the War of American Independence, in which France openly took the side of the American 'rebels', the Dutch gave much support to the Americans. The arms-smugglers on the little Dutch West Indian island of St Eustatius, nicknamed 'The Golden Rock', especially enjoyed themselves. At last the British lost patience with the Dutch and declared the Fourth (and last) Naval War on them. That war was mainly fought in European seas, but the English also sent Captain Shirley on the 'Leander' to capture the Dutch possessions on the Gold Coast. Elmina itself was too strong, but all the Dutch forts east of Elmina were captured. Only at Accra did the garrison of the fort put up any strong resistance; it was supported by the local people, especially those of their chief broker, Otu. After a prolonged bombardment in which the fort was badly damaged, the Dutch gave up and fled to Christiansborg. Chief Otu later helped the Danes with his troops in their war against the Awuna. In the peace-treaty the English signed with the Dutch in 1784, all the captured forts were given back.

For a long time afterwards Fort Crèvecoeur remained a ruin, but was rebuilt in the early nineteenth century. In 1862, however, it was once more wrecked, this time by an earthquake. The fort was partly reconstructed, and after the departure of the Dutch in 1868, named after the British administrator who had been instrumental in the Exchange of Territories of that year, Ussher. Later the British began to use Ussher Fort (as well as nearby James Fort) as a prison, and in the annals of twentieth-century Ghanaian history the building achieved a certain fame as the place where – before as well as after Independence – politicians were detained for

63

various lengths of time.

The French, to whom the American War of Independence was a victory, were after 1783 more intent than ever on getting a permanent foothold on the Gold Coast. Eventually, in 1786, they found the people of the little village of Amoku, about six miles (10 km) east of Anomabu, willing to cede them, for the considerable amount of 450 oz of gold, a patch of land, about a quarter of a mile (400 m) from the sea, to build a fort on. They called the nearest coastal town, about a mile (1·6 km) away, 'Serpent', a phonetic corruption of what the English called Saltpond. The French arrived with a lot of men, but the French 'fort' at Amoku became far from impressive: a little thatched mud building, defended with two cannon. The French royal standard, however, fluttered from its top, and the French had made their *acte de présence*. With the next store-ship, about a year later, a few more building materials arrived, but the people of Amoku continued to ask for more and more customary gifts: they declared that a stone in the centre of the fort was a 'fetish', which made the French run into further customary expenses.

After the revolution of 1789 French ships only rarely anchored at Amoku. In 1793 the new French Republic declared war on England and Holland, but the French factor at Amoku saved his skin by declaring that he was a 'royalist'. But during the second war against England, the fort was attacked by Africans in the pay of the British, and the French factor blew himself, his fort, and some of his enemies, up. Some Frenchmen, however, continued to stay at Amoku, and when in 1807 the town was attacked by the Ashanti one of the last French survivors sought refuge with the Dutch at Elmina.

7 From trade to politics: the nineteenth century

In the days of Napoleon, Holland was first made a kingdom under his brother Louis, but it was later incorporated into the French Empire. Nearly all Dutch colonies were taken by the English, who were complete masters of the seas, but it is an interesting historical detail that the only places in the world where the Dutch tricolour continued to flutter without interruption were the Dutch possessions on the Gold Coast, which the English simply did not think worth taking, and the Dutch factory on the island of Deshima, in Japan, which country did not allow any other foreign settlement in the long period of 'seclusion' (1640–1854).

Although Elmina and its subordinate settlements remained officially Dutch, all direct communications with Holland were of course cut off, and virtually all commercial activities had come to a standstill (occasionally American vessels arrived to buy some slaves). Dutch officials spent their time not only writing voluminous, often rather boring but occasionally interesting reports, but also beautifying Elmina Castle and its surroundings.

By the end of the eighteenth century the ideas of the Enlightenment were no longer the monopoly of a tiny intellectual elite, and they began also to influence areas beyond Europe: as usual, ideas followed the path of trade. One of the most important issues brought up by the Enlightenment was that of the justification of slavery and slave trade. By the middle of the century, when the slave trade was at its apogee, we see also the beginning of a change in attitudes. In the 1740s an African slave brought to the Netherlands and educated as a *predikant* (pastor) at the University of Leyden, Johannes Eliza Capiteyn, drew much support from his audiences with his theological 'proof' that the Holy Scriptures justify the enslavement of Africans. The fact that the pathetic Capiteyn (who ended his career in misery at Elmina, accused by his superiors of having reverted to paganism) thought it necessary to defend the slave trade at all is in itself a sign that people had begun to have second thoughts about the practice. Criticism grew, and fifty years later the Abolitionist Movement had become a political force to reckon with, if not in Holland, at least in England. The eventual success of the Abolitionists like Wilberforce and Clarkson was of course not due to a sudden upsurge of humanitarian public opinion alone. Faint protests against the institutions of slavery and the slave trade can be found in European literature from the sixteenth century onwards. But the loss of the American colonies considerably reduced the British slave market. The new class of British industrialists looked to Africa for raw materials and new markets for its mass-produced goods rather than for slaves. Toussaint l'Ouverture's great slave rebellion in French West Indian colony of St Domingue, leading to the foundation of the Republic of Haiti, caused a chain-reaction throughout the West Indian plantations and a general fear among the planters. But the most important single cause for the success of the Abolitionists was probably the effect of Napoleon's Continental Blockade on the sugar industry: when the European continent was cut off from the overseas world, a satisfactory surrogate for cane sugar was found in beet sugar. This does not mean that people no longer wanted cane sugar: in fact they remained for a long time prejudiced against the new surrogate. When the Napoleonic wars were over, the West Indian sugar planters still found a ready market for their product. But although the planters continued to rely on slave labour, the acquisition of new slaves became very difficult: the British Parliament made the trade in slaves illegal by an Act of 1807. The French had in fact abolished the trade in the early days of the Revolution, but Napoleon reinstated it. In 1814, after the latter's fall, they abolished it again; the Dutch, under British pressure, soon followed suit.

The demand for slaves, however, especially on the sugar plantations of Spanish Cuba, and on the cotton plantations in the South of the United States remained great. In 1807, even a few weeks before the British did so, the Americans had also abolished the slave trade, but during the entire first half of the nineteenth century a vast illegal slave trade was carried on, against which the small squadrons for the suppression of the trade were virtually powerless. In fact, during this relatively short period more slaves were smuggled across the Atlantic than in the whole era of the 'legal' slave trade. It was, as one of the 'crusaders' expressed it, 'like trying to build a dam across the mouth of a river'. Once a certain stretch of coast was under control, the slave smugglers would simply divert their activities to neighbouring areas.

One of the areas where it was not very difficult to build such a 'dam' in the stream of slaves which continued to flow out of Africa, was of course the Gold Coast with its many forts, which served as so many bases for the anti-slave trade squadrons. During the eighteenth century most forts had been adapted to the large-scale slave trade. Elmina Castle was equipped with large slave prisons, under the Governor's apartments for females and in dungeons under the seaward end of the castle for males. In smaller forts one or more bastions contained slave prisons. A typical example is the last fort the British built; the one at Beyin, whose south-west bastion, so much bigger than the other bastions, contained a slave prison.

But now different uses had to be found for the forts and castles. Initially it was hoped that the old gold trade could be revived, and to that end the active Dutch Governor Daendels,[1] a former Governor of the Dutch East Indies, sent several reconnaissance expeditions to the upper reaches of the Ankobra, Prah and Volta rivers in 1816–17. But the long years of intensive slave trade had thoroughly disrupted the gold trade and many of the traditional African mines had been abandoned. The trade in products like palm-oil, an important raw material for the soap-industry, was encouraged, but it soon became clear that the Dutch,

British and Danish possessions on the Gold Coast were no longer profitable.

At the time of the abolition of the slave trade, the Ashanti empire was in its heyday. For a long time now, slaves had been sold for arms and ammunition, which were used for the subjugation of a large number of states around the Amanto or confederation of original Ashanti states. Under Osei Bonsu (1800–1824) Ashanti reached its greatest territorial extent, stretching from Gonja in the North to the coast. The later conquered states maintained, however, a great degree of autonomy and their submission to the Asantehene was mainly expressed by the payment of an annual tribute and the stationing of a sort of military governor. Consequently there were often rebellions in these states against Ashanti authority. One such rebellion took place in the very year that the British abolished the slave trade. In that year two chiefs of Assin, Tsibu and Aputai, who were subordinate to the Asantehene, had a quarrel with another chief of Assin about a gold-theft. An Ashanti army intervened, but Tsibu and Aputai fled into Fanti territory. The Ashanti army pursued them and met with Fanti resistance. The Fanti were defeated at Abora, and many refugees, including Tsibu and Aputai, converged on Anomabu fort for protection. The Ashanti besieged the fort and only withdrew after its commander had delivered up Tsibu and Aputai, together with 1,000 refugees. In fact, the Ashanti at first demanded not less than 2,000 refugees as slaves, but after negotiations this number was brought down to 1,000. Later it appeared, however, to the great indignation of British public opinion, that the commander of Anomabu fort had sold the other 1,000 refugees to passing slave ships. This was the first Ashanti invasion of the coast, and during most of the rest of the nineteenth century the threat of a repetition of such an invasion was to remain the chief issue of coastal politics.

After the withdrawal of the Ashanti, the Fanti wanted to take revenge on the people of Accra and of Elmina, whom they suspected of being in alliance with them. Elmina in particular had a traditionally good relationship with Ashanti, and the Dutch for some time connived at the continuing slave trade, especially of the powerful mulatto trader Jan Niezer. This antagonism was not to end until the departure of the Dutch in 1872. While Cape Coast continued to be on the alert for Ashanti, Elmina remained on the alert for Fanti. In 1811 the Ashanti armies again marched towards the coast, in order to suppress a rebellion of Akim and to punish Agona for its support of Akim. A band of Akim warriors attacked Fort Lcydsaamheid at Apam to release some Fanti prisoners and found little resistance from the garrison. On their departure they threw all the cannons over the walls. The English fort at Winneba did not show itself any more resistant to Ashanti attack. Shortly afterwards, one of the British sergeants of that fort was accused of refusing to return a sum of gold which had been given to him for safe-keeping by one of the townsmen during the Ashanti invasion. The commander of the fort, Meredith, was also held responsible, and was eventually dragged off to the bush, where he died after torture. Meredith's successor in the fort was faced with a long-lasting siege by the townspeople, and eventually no other solution could be found than to evacuate it and to blow it up, after a bombardment of the town. For many years afterwards passing British captains used to fire a broadside into the town, 'in memory of the murdered whiteman'. Much later in the nineteenth century, missionaries built a church on the very site of the former British fort at Winneba.

The energetic Dutch Governor Daendels, eager to exploit to the full the existing friendly relationship between Elmina and Kumasi, sent in 1816 a mulatto ambassador, Huydecooper, a descendant of a former Director-General of Elmina, to the Ashanti capital. He was received with full honours, and made, on Daendels' behalf, a treaty with Osei Bonsu, in which it was stipulated, among other things, that the Ashanti and the Dutch were to co-operate in the construction of a highway linking Kumasi with Elmina. Fearing that all trade might be diverted to Elmina, the British Company of Merchants did not stay behind, and sent T. E. Bowdich, a nephew of Governor Hope Smith, to Kumasi for the establishment of better relations. Bowdich arrived shortly after Huydecooper's departure from the Asantehene's Court, and naturally pleased the king by signing a treaty by which his sovereignty over the coastal districts was recognised. This, of course, was unacceptable to the Fanti, who compelled Hope Smith not to comply with its terms.

In 1819 the British Government decided to intervene by sending an ambassador of its own, Joseph Dupuis. Dupuis was an able negotiator, who during a prolonged stay at Kumasi managed to get the full co-operation of the Asantehene, but the Cape Coast merchants regarded him with deep suspicion. In 1821 the Crown took over from the Committee of Merchants, and the Gold Coast then came under the administration of Governor MacCarthy, who was stationed in Sierra Leone. MacCarthy, however, failed to follow up the agreement which Dupuis had made in Kumasi, and when in 1823 the Ashanti once more marched South, MacCarthy marched up to meet them, but was killed in an ambush. The British had their revenge when two years later they routed the main Ashanti army on the Accra plains.

In 1828 the British Government decided to abandon the Gold Coast, as it cost too much to maintain. The merchants in Cape Coast protested that prospects for a revival of trade, at that time when peace seemed secure, were better than ever. Eventually a solution was found by putting the British forts under the authority of a Committee of London Merchants with a parliamentary grant. Captain George Maclean as 'President' on the Coast was sent out. Having no mercantile interests, Maclean was thought to be the best man to manage the affairs of the committee and indeed proved his worth. He arranged a peace between Ashanti and the coastal states, in which the former gave up most of its claims on the coast, and trade quickly resumed. Maclean was also the first European to exercise some real jurisdiction outside the walls of the forts, by asking chiefs of the immediate hinterland to bring their cases before him and by encouraging the application of British law to their 'palavers'. Maclean also re-occupied a number of out-forts which had been abandoned.

But there was in Maclean's successful administration (1830–42) one serious crisis of a personal character. He was married to a poetess famous in those days, Letitia E. Langdon, better known by her initials 'L.E.L.', who came to join him at Cape Coast Castle. Not long after her arrival, however, this romantic lady died suddenly, in somewhat doubtful circumstances. She probably died of an overdose of a sedative, but many of her distressed Victorian readers were ready to suspect foul play on the part of her husband. The limelight now fell on Maclean, who was soon cleared of suspicion of having murdered his wife, but whose policies were now more closely scrutinised. One of the most serious charges was that he had connived at illegal slave-dealing practices. A Commission of Inquiry was set up and in 1841 a Select Committee under Dr Madden assessed his administration. Maclean was cleared of all blame and it appeared that in fact the Merchant Committee had been doing unexpectedly well; in 1843 the Crown once more took over. Maclean was maintained as Judicial Assessor till his death in 1847. A simple stone slab marked 'G.M.' next to a similar slab marked 'L.E.L.'[2] in the middle of the 'parade' of Cape Coast Castle marks the place where these two people are buried. A few yards away is yet another slab marked 'P.Q.', for the Rev Philip Quarcoe, the Oxford-trained African minister and teacher who was the castle's chaplain for nearly fifty years to 1816.

In 1844 the new Governor on behalf of the Crown, Hill, signed with the chiefs of some states of the coast and the immediate interior an agreement known as 'the Bond', whereby they accepted British jurisdiction; this was the beginning of British colonisation of the Gold Coast in a modern sense. Running the colony, defending it against the permanent threat of Ashanti invasions – between 1811 and 1874 there were no less than seven clashes between the Ashanti and the British – and in particular the maintenance of the forts were all very expensive, and the Colonial Office tried to find means of recovering part of the costs. The

Danes had for some time been considering the sale of their possessions of the Gold Coast (together with Tranquebar on the south-east coast of India). Although they had started plantations inland from 1788 onwards, first as an alternative to shipping slaves to the inhuman conditions of the New World, and afterwards to try to make up for the losses they suffered by their abandonment of the slave-trade in 1803, these had proved generally unsuccessful. The death-rate at Christiansborg had risen terribly, perhaps as a result of the sleeping-sickness to which the Danes must have been exposed inland, and between 1830 and 1840 no less than six successive governors died at their posts. They also had the expense of maintaining the chain of forts from Christiansborg east of Keta; they became involved in numerous minor wars in their attempt to enforce the ban on the slave-trade; other trade was at a low ebb, and the establishments were operating at a considerable loss.

The British, though faced with much the same problems, did not wish to see the Danish forts fall into French or Belgian hands, which appeared to be the alternative to British purchase; they wished to stamp out slave-smuggling (Keta was a notorious den of slavers); and they wanted to be able to enforce the collection of poll-tax. In 1850 long negotiations culminated in Denmark selling her five Gold Coast forts to Britain for £10,000.

After this the British tried to reach an agreement with the Dutch for the levy of uniform import duties. Attempts to levy poll-tax in the areas under British jurisdiction failed on the whole and only led to numerous wrangles with the Dutch about the ill-defined extent of those areas, the Dutch by that time also claiming to have considerable zones of influence. In 1865 a Select Committee under Colonel Ord once more proposed that the British withdraw from the Gold Coast, but again the merchant community protested. Instead, the British reached an agreement with the Dutch in 1867 whereby the two nations would exchange a number of forts so that the British would control a continuous strip of coast east of the Sweet River (between Cape Coast and Elmina) and the Dutch one west of that river. In 1868 Mori,

Cormantin, Apam, Senya Bereku, and Dutch Accra became British and British Komenda, Sekondi, Dixcove and Beyin became Dutch. This arrangement would make the levy of duties and administration much simpler, but unfortunately the Europeans had 'forgotten' to inform the people whom it most affected of their scheme. The people of the former British Komenda in particular protested vehemently, and called on their Fanti allies for a war on Elmina.

The Dutch Government felt obliged to send a military expedition.[3] Law and order were somewhat restored, but the root-cause of continued antagonism — the lack of interest the Dutch had for so long been showing in their 'Possessions on the Coast of Guinea' – remained. The fort at Dixcove was named after one of the gun-boats which had been sent from the Netherlands, 'Metalen Kruis' (Metal Cross) and the fort at Beyin after the King, 'Willem III', but not much else was done. The cost of maintaining the 'Dutch possessions' was cause for great concern in the Netherlands. Soon the Dutch started negotiations with the British for a transfer of their possessions, and in 1872 a treaty was signed to that effect, whereby the British paid the Dutch the nominal sum of £3,790 1s. 6½d. for the stores and fixtures in the Dutch forts, and gave up some claims they had in Northern Sumatra, at the same time giving the Dutch the right to recruit coolies in India to work in Surinam, where the plantations were in rapid decline after the abolition of slavery there in 1863. The people of Elmina protested vehemently against the proposed transfer, and even sent, at their own expense, an ambassador to The Hague to plead their cause, but the Dutch Minister of Colonies would not even receive him. On 6 April, 1872, the Dutch flag was at last lowered for ever from Elmina Castle.

Clearly, during the nineteenth century the function of the forts changed completely. The Europeans no longer relied on them to protect their national commercial interests. In fact one can hardly speak of any commercial rivalry among the European nations on the Gold Coast in the nineteenth century. The accent was now more than ever on their military value, on the one hand to serve as naval bases or even refuelling stations,[4] on the other to protect European interests against African attacks. The Europeans now began to look far beyond the walls of their forts. The Danes were the first to establish plantations at a considerable distance from their forts,[5] and the English and Dutch followed their example. The Dutch also tried to open a gold-mine in their 'Ahanta Protectorate', but none of these enterprises proved very successful. The Danish and British missionary activities proved more successful: the Dutch were in this respect virtually inactive.

Of course no new trade forts were built in the nineteenth century, but some of the existing ones were modernised, especially in their armament. At Elmina and Cape Coast some new fortifications were also built to protect the castles and the towns against respectively Fanti and Ashanti attacks. Already in the early eighteenth century, in the days of unrest caused by the Komenda wars, the first of these outposts had been built on a hill a few hundred yards north-west of Cape Coast Castle. This little round tower mounted seven guns and covered the approaches to the castle and part of the town. It was named after its builder Phipps' Tower. Later in that century the building fell into ruins. In 1837, however, it was rebuilt as a very small but strong fort, and named after Queen Victoria, who came to the throne in that year. It is still in good condition. It was the last and most westerly of the three defence-works which were built in those days to protect Cape Coast Castle. The other two were Smith's Tower, built in 1819–20 under Governor Hope-Smith, and Fort McCarthy, built shortly after the arrival in the country of the Governor of that name. Of the last fort very little is left, but Smith's Tower was reconstructed in more durable materials in the 1830s and has served since those days as the Cape Coast Lighthouse. It also changed names, and is now known as Fort William.

At Elmina, where Fort Coenraadsburg gave good coverage to the castle, the town, or rather the towns, were frequently attacked by the Fanti. In the nineteenth century

'Elmina Newtown' on the left bank of the Benya river, which is now modern Elmina, developed rapidly, and during the nineteenth century a whole series of defence works was built in a wide ring around it. The first of these redoubts, Fort Beekestein, on a bluff on the left bank of the river, was probably built in the very first years of the nineteenth century. In 1811, during the Fanti siege of that year, another redoubt was built at the point where the rocky coastline changes into a sandy beach, where canoes can land. At this point also must have ended the defensive moat which in earlier years had been built across the peninsula between the Benya and the sea, to protect the old Elmina town which was situated on it. This redoubt, originally called Fort Waakzaamheid (Vigilance), became better known as 'Veersche Schans', De Veer's redoubt, as it was built in the days of Governor De Veer. It is probably also from those days that the well-preserved round watchtower dates which was built at the other end of Elmina, in the Government Gardens. Originally the castle garden was situated closer to the castle, at the foot of St Jago Hill, but gradually Elmina Newtown must have encroached on it. Especially in the difficult years after the abolition of the West India Company, when very few ships arrived with fresh supplies, the inhabitants of the castle must have depended heavily on the products of the garden, and a new garden was made at the north-eastern end of the town, where the watch-tower gave a good view over the marshlands stretching towards Cape Coast, in which many a battle was fought between the people of Elmina and the Fanti.

Near the Government Garden, on the corner of the modern Liverpool Street and Marblestone Street, there was also a 'Heeren Sociëteit' or Gentlemen's Club, which has become memorable because it was there in 1808 that some people of Elmina murdered President Hoogenboom while he was playing billiards. Governor Hoogenboom had made himself much hated among the Elmina community by his disorderly and arbitrary behaviour. At least he got a proper funeral; he was the first Governor to be buried in the monumental mausoleum which was built in 1806 in a new graveyard, still known as the 'Dutch Cemetery'.

Two hills north of St Jago Hill, originally known as the 'Coebergh' and the 'Catoenbergh' (Cow Hill and Cotton Hill), are in fact higher than St Jago Hill and were also provided with redoubts. The square redoubt on the Coebergh (on which the Catholic Mission School now stands) probably dates from the 1820s and was reconstructed and reinforced in 1843. It was called 'Fort Schomerus' after the Governor of those days. Cotton Hill to the east had a round redoubt, which was rebuilt in 1855 as Fort Java. The foundation stone with the inscription 'Februarij 1855 – Java' can still be seen in the wall of the Guard Room of Elmina Castle. This redoubt was called by that name, because at that time the former Cotton Hill had already become known as Java Hill (as it still is today), as it was there that many of the African recruits of the Royal Dutch East Indian Army settled after their return from service in that colony. The recruitment of these African soldiers for 'Java' (a misnomer really: Java was the most important island of the Dutch East Indies, but these soldiers were mostly used to fight wars of 'pacification' on other islands of the archipelago) started in 1837 with considerable success in both Elmina and Kumasi. But soon it became an issue of controversy with the British, who accused the Dutch of engaging in the illicit slave trade in disguise; in fact, the Dutch bought at their 'Recruitment Depots' slaves whom they manumitted from the moment of their purchase, but on condition that they sign at the same time a contract for six or twelve years' military service in the East Indies and redeem the price paid for their 'freedom' out of their pay. This recruitment was suspended in 1842, but resumed in the 1860s. In fact, a few days after the official transfer of Elmina to the British, in 1872, a last Dutch ship with African 'Java Recruits' was allowed to leave. These ex-servicemen often brought on their return from the East Javanese *batik* or wax-print cloth with them, which greatly appealed to the local taste. Soon Dutch textile factories began to produce imitation *batik* cotton prints on a large scale especially for the West African market, and 'Java Wax Print' has come to stay as one of the most popular kinds of cloth in the whole of West Africa and is now produced not only in Holland, but also in other countries, including Ghana itself.

A last fairly large redoubt was built in 1868 near the coast east of Elmina, as a kind of counterpart to the De Veer redoubt, and was named after Governor Nagtglas. A stone similar to the one commemorating the Java redoubt can also be found in the wall opposite the one in which the first one is set. In translation it says: 'The last stone laid by Colonel C. J. M. Nagtglas, Commissioner of the Netherlands Government and Governor of these Possessions, Elmina, 28th September, 1869.' This stone does not commemorate, as is sometimes believed, the departure of the Dutch, which took place two and a half years later; to the contrary: in spite of the troubles in which they were involved, at that time the Dutch still hoped for a bright future for their West African colony.

All these nineteenth century redoubts and fortifications were of course of a purely military character. So were the few forts which were eventually built in the interior by the British. Hoping to avoid a repetition of the events after the ill-fated exchange treaty of 1868, the British and Dutch decided to inform the African parties concerned in good time of the proposed transfer of the Dutch possessions to the British. One of these parties was the Asantehene Kofi Karikari, who maintained that he had a claim on Elmina, based on a 'note' which his ancestor Osei Tutu had acquired after the conquest of Denkyira. A lot of confusion developed on the subject of this 'note', and at one stage it seemed that the Asantehene was willing to give up his claim. But shortly after the transfer, large Ashanti armies once more marched down to the coast. On the approach of their Ashanti allies the people of Elmina once more took courage, and decided to join the invaders. The new British occupants of the castle issued an ultimatum that the people of Elmina should deliver up their arms at the castle, but it was ignored. The ancient Elmina town was then bombarded from the castle, and virtually razed to the ground. It has never been rebuilt, and the large open space on the peninsula in front of the castle, which once housed nearly 20,000 people, remains as eloquent testimony to this event.

The immediate result of this Ashanti invasion was the 'Sagrenti War', in which a British army under Sir Garnet Wolseley marched up to Kumasi and burnt the city (1874). In the Treaty of Fomena of the same year, the Asantehene gave up all jurisdiction over the states in the area south of the Prah and Offin rivers, which became known as the Gold Coast Colony, and promised to keep the trade-routes open, to abolish human sacrifice, and to pay a heavy indemnity of 50,000 oz of gold. Shortly afterwards Kofi Karikari was destooled, and so was his successor, in 1883, for not pursuing a sufficiently aggressive policy in the subsequent years.

In the early '90s the effects of the new imperialism of the Berlin colonial conference began to be felt. The British feared that their zone of influence to the north of the Gold Coast was seriously threatened by an enclosure of German influence from Togo in the east and French influence from Ivory Coast in the west. In 1896 the British felt the need to establish a Resident in Kumasi. The Ashanti, however, rightly feared that this was only the first step towards British annexation of the kingdom, and tried to prevent this by sending at their own expense a delegation to London. Nevertheless, the British sent an ultimatum, and when the only answer from Kumasi, arriving a few days after the ultimatum had expired, was that a delegation had been sent to England, an expeditionary force under Major Baden-Powell (the founder of the Boy Scouts) was sent to Kumasi to install the Resident by force. Kumasi was occupied, the Asantehene, Prempeh I, accused of not having fulfilled the terms of the Treaty of Fomena, offered his submission, claiming 'the protection of the Queen of England'. As Prempeh was not able to supply the 50,000 oz of gold demanded in the treaty, he and a number of members of the royal household were brought as prisoners to the coast. Prempeh stayed for four years as a prisoner in Elmina Castle, where he and his household occupied the two square towers on top of the seaward bastions. Eventually, in 1899, the royal prisoners were exiled to the Seychelle Islands whence they returned only in 1931.

In Kumasi the construction started of a big military fort, mainly of swish, which was to house the Resident. For a few years all remained quiet, although the Ashanti soon saw that the British were encroaching more and more on their autonomy. In 1900 Governor Hodgson, on a visit to Kumasi, had the bad taste to demand the surrender of the Golden Stool, the soul of the Ashanti state, even expressing his desire to sit on it, something that nobody, not even the Asantehene himself, could ever do. This was the last straw; all the pent-up resentment of the humiliated Ashanti burst out in a popular revolt known as the Yaa Asantewa War, after the Queen Mother of Ejisu.

For several months Hodgson, his entourage, and his African allies were closely besieged in the fort. All communications were severed when the new telegraph link with the coast was cut; the British, very shortsightedly, had entirely relied on this modern means of communication, without considering its inherent fragility. Hundreds of people died in and around the isolated fort. Hodgson and a small party managed to escape, however, and to inform Accra. A month later, a new expeditionary force, sent from the coast, released the remaining garrison in Kumasi fort and subdued Yaa Asantewa and her followers. Some of the war-leaders were also exiled to the Seychelles. Kumasi Fort has been well preserved and is now a military museum.

Meanwhile the British had sent their famous mulatto surveyor Ferguson (from Anomabu) with a small armed force to the Ashanti hinterland, where he diligently staked out the British claim on what was to become the 'Northern Territories'. In the north-west they had to cope not only with the threat of French expansionism, but also with the more real danger of attacks by the well-equipped armies of the famous Samory. As this expeditionary force was rather small, it needed some well defended bases. For that purpose small forts were built at Wa and Bole in 1897. It was at Wa Fort, which still exists, that Ferguson died, after having been wounded in a skirmish with Samory's men.

With the construction of these last two forts the long history of the building of forts and castles in Ghana came to an end.

1 In 1790 the 'soul-less body' of the Dutch West India Company had at last collapsed, and after an intermediary period in which councils of various names had taken over government, its former possessions were from 1814 administered directly by the Ministry of Trade and Colonies of the new Kingdom of the Netherlands.

2 Letitia Langdon is not the only English lady whose death at Cape Coast Castle has been commemorated in a tombstone. On the platform at the west end of the spur is a stone on which 'the Governor and Gentlemen of this Settlement' expressed their 'unfeigned sorrow and regard' at the death of Mrs Eliza Fountaine, wife of an English clerk; she died on 26 August 1803.

3 The second in the nineteenth century: in 1837 a quarrel with Nana Badoe Bonsu II, King of Ahanta, had led to the death of two Dutch officers at Butri, followed by the total rout and death of Governor Tonneboeijer and thirty of his men by Ahanta warriors, after which a 'punitive expedition' was sent against Ahanta, leading to the establishment of the Dutch 'Ahanta Protectorate'.

4 At Axim the Dutch leased a coal-station to the French Navy for some time.

5 Of these early Danish plantations the first one, 'Fredriksnopel', founded in 1788 by the Rev Isert near Akropong in Akwapim, was perhaps the most daring and idealistic enterprise, leading to the earliest missionary activities in Ghana. In later years several other plantations were established, at the foot of the Akwapim hills, directly north of Osu, and a few near the mouth of the Volta. Of these plantations only the one called Dacubie, founded in 1808, produced for some time commercial quantities of coffee and cotton. Some ruins of plantation houses still survive, such as that of Fredriksgave (1830) near the village of Sesenfi and Dacubie, about three miles (5 km) to the NE of it. Another interesting feature still reminding us of this episode are the rows of tamarind trees planted by the Danes as can still be seen along Salem road in Accra, which once formed the avenue leading to the plantation Fredriksberg, or, more impressively, at the village of Kpongkpo, just north of Abokobi at the foot of the Akwapim hills.

8 Life in and around the forts

Finally, one may ask what kind of people used to live in the forts, and what kind of lives they led there. Of course there were differences in the regulations governing one fort or the other, but we may attempt a general outline.

The Europeans who came to the coast in the service of the companies were either commercial, military or professional men. Among the employees of the companies on the Coast, many were not of the nationality of that company. Even the highest posts were sometimes occupied by foreigners: so we find for instance an agent of the Royal African Company with the Dutch name of Blaeu, or a Director-General of the Dutch West India Company with the English name of William Butler. Others came from Germany, Sweden, France or even Turkey; but it is often rather difficult to recognise the true nationalities, as foreign names were mostly 'translated'. These foreigners often gave a pretty hard job to the clerks who had to do their correspondence. The companies also constantly had a large number of slaves in their service, the so-called 'castle slaves', some of whom were quite able craftsmen. They mostly lived in huts outside the castles and forts, earned small wages and worked their farms when not engaged in work for the company. Their condition resembled that of 'domestic slavery', long a feature of African society, and was of course completely different from the inhuman treatment to which slaves on the West Indian plantations were subjected.

The hierarchy in personnel and the daily routine in the forts and castles were very similar to those on board ship. The position of the commander of a fort was like that of the captain of a ship at anchor. Life was regulated according to the hour-glass, and bells rang day and night to mark the hours and the times for the change of the guard. Particularly in the castles and the big forts, a relatively large proportion of the garrison was of a purely military character and included professional gunners, drummers and trumpeters. There were many professional tradesmen, like blacksmiths, carpenters and coopers, and only a relatively small proportion of the men were engaged in purely commercial activities.

Much slave labour was used in the loading and unloading of the ships. Canoes and surf-boats formed the essential link between shore and ship, and canoe-men – mostly freemen from Elmina – were held in high esteem. Only Elmina Castle could be approached by small sea-going craft: the mouth of the Benya, protected against silting by a short breakwater, formed a kind of small deep-sea port, which boasted a real quay and the unique (wooden) crane of the Gold Coast. Communications between the forts were generally maintained by small coastal vessels ('yachts') whose components, prefabricated in Europe, were assembled at places like Dixcove, Butri and Elmina. Surprisingly, the Europeans remained for a long time reluctant to use African timber, and even for the construction of forts large quantities of European oak were imported. Timber, now one of the most important exports of Ghana, never figured on the ancient cargo-lists. Occasionally Europeans travelled over land, particularly when travelling from the 'leeward' to the 'windward', in which case they were carried, like their rich or powerful African counterparts, in a hammock borne on the heads of two or four slaves, accompanied by a train of carriers with their head-loads.

Many people were constantly engaged in maintenance and repair work on the buildings. Particularly the British forts were of a rather weak construction, often built with large quantities of swish and stones, occasionally with soft locally burnt brick. In 1755, during the construction of Anomaboe Fort, a kiln was made there, and the company's slaves, trained in brickmaking, are reported to have made more than 15,000 bricks a day. Admittedly, they were 'not so good for outside work, but equally good for arching and inside work . . . and they cost nothing to the Company, as they are made by Slaves'.

A Cape Coast diary of 1780 gives an idea of activities in the Castle on a morning in May:

. . . Saturday 29th May. 8 a.m. Capt. Lysaught arrived in a seven hand Canoe from Tantum whence he hath desired to leave to go for Change of Air. The Coy.'s Slaves & Mumford pawns were in number 96 employ'd this Week, 41 men & boys and 49 Women & girls. The seven Bricklayers are at Work on the new Building to secure it before the Rains, hourly expected. Three Men are blowing Stone, four Carpenters making accommodation ladder work to keep an easy Communication between the East and West Bastions. Three Blacksmiths making Canoe staples & other Work in the Castle. Six Coopers making Liquor Measures, securing empty Caskes by heading them up, attending the Liquor. Three Armourers cleaning Arms. Two Boys attending in the Hall. Two Labourers mixing Mortar. Of the Canoe men seven went to Dixcove on Sunday – the others are cleaning the Channel from Mud, or the Garden would be overflowed when the Rains set in. Two Bomboys to take care [while] six Labourers work in the Garden and the Stockyard. Cudjoe, the Slaves' Bomboy went with ten Women to cut & carry Wood. Ten to carry Stone & Water to the Bricklayers. Twelve to sweep the Hall, the Gentlemen's Appartments, Offices, Hospital, &c., &c. . . .

Roofs in particular often needed repairs. When steep gabled roofs were abolished and transformed into flat ones, a rather cumbersome technique was used: a layer of bricks was laid in a parquet-pattern on top of a ceiling of boards, and cemented in order to make it waterproof. During the dry season cracks would develop in this cement[1] and rot would set in during the wet season. Consequently these heavy roof-constructions often had to be replaced.

Clerks must have had a big task. In those days, before the

invention of the typewriter and carbon-paper, they were engaged in making endless numbers of copies of letters, which themselves were written in a very cumbersome style: much energy was expended on polite phraseology and calligraphy. Accountancy was no simpler; the basic unit of accountancy was the ounce of gold, but there were different rates for use in Europe and on the Coast. Rates of exchange had to be constantly adjusted. Certain goods might be much in demand for a short time, but in those days in which returning mail often took more than a year, by the time those goods arrived, very often the demand had diminished, and store-keepers and book-keepers had to revalue the whole stock. For their commercial transactions with indigenous traders the Europeans generally relied on African *'makelaers'* or 'brokers', often rich local merchants, many of whom were related to the chiefs. These 'brokers' fulfilled an important political role. They mediated between the companies and the traditional authorities and brought the principal indigenous traders to the fort, where transactions were generally made in the courtyard or in the 'House of Trade'. Every time the forts were supplied with merchandise from the headquarters, gold, slaves and other products bought since the last time the fort had been supplied with European goods were collected and returned to the headquarters. In Elmina only the Chief Merchant had a key to the company's gold-chest.

Informal contacts with the surrounding African communities were on the whole very limited, and after the departure of the Portuguese, attempts to bring education and the Christian religion to the African communities were at best sporadic. During the daytime the Europeans strayed occasionally into the African townships, but the company rules forbade them, on strict penalties, to spend the night there. Yet, many a company official took an African wife, and the fathers of children born out of such unions were compelled by law to pay for their upkeep and some education. Several families in places like Elmina, Cape Coast and Accra still carry the names of seventeenth and eighteenth century company officials. Often the mulatto offspring of these officials took service with the companies in which several of them reached high positions.

The mulatto communities have played an important role in Ghana's history. Although comparatively much smaller than similar communities on the other side of the Atlantic, they were on the whole more vociferous and in many respects they formed the nucleus of the later coastal elite. They formed some important trading families. Some of them followed the Christian and European patrilineal system, hence the persistence of various European surnames, while others were absorbed into traditional Akan matrilineal society. The most successful of these traders built some impressive establishments like the 'Little Fort' of the Brew family at Anomabu or the Richter house at Osu, originally built with bastions, like a fort.

There was not much possibility for recreation: drinking was often the only outlet. The only outing for the men in Elmina and Cape Coast was a walk in the respective Government Gardens, or, on occasions, canoeing on the Sweet River (Kakum), between the two towns; there were still fewer opportunities for the men in small forts such as those at Apam or Prampram. No surprise therefore, that there were frequent brawls between these bored or drunken men. There are at least two cases known of Director-Generals at Elmina who drank themselves literally to death, in their last days making life unendurable for their subordinates in the castle. One of them is known to have thrown cannon-balls at his Fiscal and afterwards to have kicked him so hard in the sides that he died a few days later. The other locked his Chief Merchant in a cage, like a wild beast, from time to time throwing bones through the bars for him to gnaw. This Director-General also bombarded Elmina town for no clear reason, after which the castle was besieged by the townspeople for several weeks (1739). In 1803 Cape Coast Castle was also besieged, after a quarrel between the townspeople and an English merchant.

It is no surprise that again and again the Governors issued circulars denouncing the widespread drinking, swearing and whoring, exhorting the men to lead a more godly life.

85

Non-attendance at church services, at least twice a week, was also punished. Officials sometimes denounced each other before the directors in Amsterdam, but a bookkeeper at Elmina, in 1703, had his defence ready: '. . . I readily admit that I do from time to time drink a good glass of wine, and also that I generally take in the morning a little glass of brandy or other *liqueur de canaille*; but I would like to know a person in this melancholy land who doesn't do that; it is even necessary for the very preservation of one's health . . .'

Discipline in the forts was thus rather strict; not only because of their basically military character, but also because it was not always the best kind of people who were prepared to take service on that notorious Coast of Guinea which became known as 'the Whiteman's Grave'. The companies probably did not dig very deep into the life-histories of the men who offered their services before engaging them. Many must have been rootless men who were out for quick money. Lack of family ties may also have rendered some men more adventurous, like the orphan David Van Nyendael who stayed for more than a year in Kumasi and part of whose estate was in fact returned to the Municipal Orphanage of Amsterdam by the company, after his death at Elmina.

Company servants, in particular those in the lowest ranks, were severely punished for the smallest offences. In Elmina, Fort Coenraadsburg served as a prison for European offenders. The death-penalty, which was in frequent use, was hardly ever applied to those in the upper ranks. The death-sentence would be carried out on the 'Gallows Battery', and the corpse of the victim would be left unburied on top of St Jago Hill 'for the birds of prey'.

Most of those who died however, were victims of the fatal 'distempers' which made the area so notorious, such as the 'land-fever' (malaria or yellow fever) or the 'red runs' (dysentery). Initially these men used to be buried within the precincts of the castles, but soon more room was needed, and in the nineteenth century European cemeteries were opened outside the castles in Elmina, Cape Coast and Accra. Thus, life at the forts in the company days must indeed have been pretty 'short and brutish', most of the time utterly boring, but occasionally hectic, as in times of war.

In the nineteenth century the inhabitants of the forts gradually broke their isolation from the surrounding world. Although the great guns became more and more rusty through lack of use and maintenance, life within the walls continued to be organised along essentially military lines. But intercourse with the people living beyond the walls tended to become more frequent and relaxed. Not only mulatto merchants but also independent Europeans began to build solid and spacious mansions in the towns surrounding the forts and castles; many interesting examples of these can still be seen. In the 1850s Cape Coast boasted already an agricultural show, and soon missionaries came to build their churches and mission houses. By 1900 the accent of European activity had completely shifted away from the forts, which by then had lost most of their utility when even government offices were opened outside their walls. They fell generally into rapid decay, and some of them suffered quite haphazard and often ugly alterations and additions like the wooden resthouses and offices which the colonial authorities built on top of some of the ruins.

In the 1950s, however, the forts and castles began to enjoy renewed interest: following the O'Neil report of 1951 and the recommendations based on the thorough research of Professor A. W. Lawrence – who wrote a standard work on the subject – the Monuments and Relics Commission (now known as the Monuments Division of the Ghana Museums and Monuments Board) set out to restore systematically these ancient buildings. Several of these restorations are now successfully completed, and most of the forts are open to the public. Some house government offices – the most obvious example is of course Christiansborg Castle, which is the seat of the Government of the Republic and which can only be visited by special permission – and others are still in use as prisons, but it is the intention of the Monuments Board to turn most of them into simple resthouses, where the modern visitor can have a taste of what it was like to live in such a building, be it for a shorter time, and in greater comfort than in the days of old!

1 Most cement was a kind of mortar made locally from shells. Mixed with ground chips of roof-tiles and bricks it was called 'tarrass', a more expensive, but more durable material. There were often quarrels about the rights to collect shells in places like Takoradi, or Nyinyanu between Accra and Senya Bereku, where they could be found in great quantities.

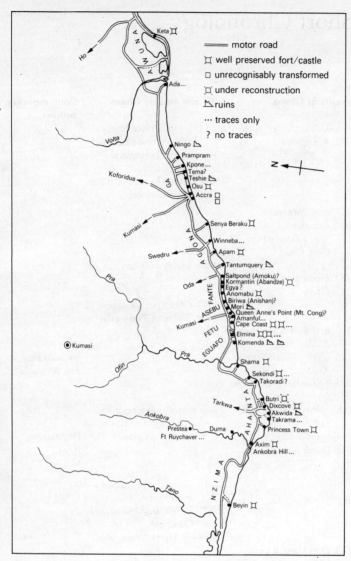

Map of the coast of Ghana, showing the forts and castles
in their present condition

Short Chronology

Events in Ghana	Events outside Ghana	Contemporary authors
14th–15th centuries: Akan migrations	1430–1460 Prince Henry the Navigator patronises early Portuguese explorers	
	1450–1500 heyday of Italian Renaissance	
1471 first Portuguese commercial transactions on the Gold Coast		
	1479 Treaty of Alcaçovas	
1482 foundation of Elmina Castle		
	1492 Columbus' discovery	
	1494 Treaty of Tordesillas	
1503 first Portuguese fort at Axim		
1515 foundation of Fort S. Antonio, Axim		Pacheco Pereira Leo Africanus
1523(?) foundation of Shama fort		
16th century: early French and English competition	16th century: Reformation, counter-reformation, wars of religion	De Marees
1612 Dutch fort at Mori		Brun Müller
	1618 Company of Guynney and Binney	
	1621 Dutch West Indian Company	
	1618–48 Thirty Years' War	
1625 Dutch attack on Elmina fails		
1631 English fort at Kormantin		
1637–42 Portuguese expelled from Gold Coast. Dutch capture Elmina, Shama, Axim		
	1648–54 Dutch driven from Brazil	

Events in Ghana	Events outside Ghana	Contemporary authors
1649–58 Caerlof's Swedish and Danish enterprises		
	1655 English capture Jamaica	
	1661 Company of Royal Adventurers	
1664–65 expeditions of Holmes and De Ruyter. Cape Coast Castle	1665–68 2nd Anglo-Dutch Naval War	Dapper
	1670–1713 Wars of Louis XIV	
	1672 Royal African Company	
	1674 New West Indian Company	
1680 Akwamu conquest of Accra	1680 Brandenburg Africa Company	
1683 Fort Gross Friedrichsburg (Princes Town)		• Barbot
1690s Komenda Wars. Rise of Ashanti under Osei Tutu, Okomfo Anokye		Phillips
1701 Ashanti defeats Denkyira	1701–1713 War of the Spanish succession. Louis XIV claims Spanish Asiento. French fort at Whydah	
1702 Fort St Louis at Assini destroyed		Bosman
1704–11 Sir Dalby Thomas, Agent at Cape Coast. Anglo-Dutch antagonism.		
	1720 Financial crashes London/Paris	Smith
1725–30 Decline of Akwamu. Forts at Tema, Prampram, Ningo, Keta	1725–40 Rise of Dahomey	Snelgrave
	1740–48 War of the Austrian Succession	
1756 French attack on Cape Coast; French fort at Anomabu	1756–63 Seven Years' War	
1765 Fort at Beyin (Apollonia)		Römer

Events in Ghana	Events outside Ghana	Contemporary authors
	1776–1783 American War of Independence	
1783–87 Forts at Ada, Keta and Teshi		
1786–1820 Danish plantations		Isert
	1789 French Revolution	
1807 first Ashanti invasion of the coast	1807 British Abolition of Slave Trade Act	
	1815 Battle of Waterloo	
1816–18 missions Huydecooper, Bowdich, Dupuis to Kumasi		Bowdich Dupuis
	1830 July Revolution	
1831–47 George Maclean		
	1848 Communist Manifesto	
1851 Sale of Danish possessions to England		
1868 Anglo-Dutch exchange of territories		Cruickshank
	1870 Franco-Prussian War	
1872 Sale of Dutch possessions to England		
1873 Bombardment of Elmina		
	1884 Berlin Conference	
1896 Destruction of Kumasi and construction of Kumasi fort		
1900 Yaa Asantewa War		

A Short Bibliography

A: Books by authors mentioned in the column 'Contemporary authors' in the short chronology (most of these books are of course not easily available, but can be considered as primary sources).

Pacheco Pereira: *Esmeraldo de Situ Orbis*, Portuguese, 1508, ed. by R. Mauny in French, Bissau, 1956 and in English by G. H. T. Kimble, Hakluyt Society, 1937

Leo Africanus, original text in Arabic, 1526, ed. by A. Epaulard as *Description de l'Afrique*, Paris, 1956

P. de Marees: *Beschryvinghe ende Historische Verhael van het Gout-Coninckryck van Gunea*, 1602, partly translated in S. Purchas: *Purchas his Pilgrimage*, London, 1613

S. Brun: *Schifahrten, 6. Raisz*, Basel, 1624

O. Dapper: *Naeukeurige Beschryvinge der Africaensche Gewesten*, Amsterdam, 1668, transl. in French, 1686

W. M. Müller: *Die Afrikanische auf der Guinesischen Goldcüste gelegene Landschafft Fetu*, Hamburg, 1676

J. Barbot: *Description of the South and North Coasts of Guinea*, London, 1681

T. Phillips: *A Journal of a Voyage Made in the Hannibal in 1693–94 to Guinea*, in *Churchill's Collection of Voyages*, vol. vi, London, 1732

W. Bosman: *Naauwkeurige Beschryving van de Guinese Gout, Tand en Slavekust*, Amsterdam, 1703, publ. in English as *A New and Accurate Description of the Coast of Guinea* in 1705 and later (last ed. 1967)

W. Smith: *A Voyage to Guinea in 1726*, in T. Astley, *A New Collection of Voyages & Travels*, London, 1745

W. Snelgrave: *A New Account of Some Parts of Guinea and the Slave Trade*, London, 1734

L. F. Rømer: *Tilfaeladig Efterretning om Kysten Guinea*, Copenhagen, 1760, transl. as *Nachrichte von der Küste Guinea*, Leipzig, 1767

P. E. Isert: *Reise nach Guinea und den Caribäischen Inseln*, Copenhagen, · 1788

T. E. Bowdich: *Mission from Cape Coast Castle to Ashantee*, London, 1819

J. Dupuis: *Journal of a Residence in Ashantee*, London, 1824

B. Cruickshank: *Eighteen Years on the Gold Coast of Africa*, London, 1853

B. A small selection of modern, more easily available books:

A. A. Boahen: *Topics in West African History*, London, 1964

J. W. Blake: *Europeans in West Africa, 1450–1650*, London, 1942

C. R. Boxer: *The Dutch Seaborne Empire*, London, 1965

—— *The Portuguese Seaborne Empire*, London, 1967

W. W. Claridge: *A History of the Gold Coast and Ashanti*, London, 1915

D. Coombs: *The Gold Coast, Britain and the Netherlands, 1850–1873*, London, 1963

K. Y. Daaku: *Trade and Politics on the Gold Coast, 1600–1720*, Oxford, 1970

K. G. Davies: *The Royal African Company*, London, 1958

J. D. Fage: *Ghana, A Historical Interpretation*, Madison, 1959

J. K. Fynn: *Asante and its Neighbours, 1700–1807*, London, 1971

M. A. Kwamena-Poh: *Government and Politics in the Akuapem State, 1730–1850*, London, 1973

A. W. Lawrence: *Trade Castles and Forts of West Africa*, London, 1963

G. E. Metcalfe: *Maclean of the Gold Coast*

G. Norregard: *Danish Settlements in West Africa, 1658–1850*, Boston, 1966

J. H. Parry: *The Age of Reconnaissance*, London, 1963

M. Priestly: *West African Trade and Coast Society*, London, 1969

C. C. Reindorf: *The History of the Gold Coast and Asante*, 2nd ed., Accra, 1966

W. E. F. Ward: *A History of Ghana*, London, 1958

INDEX

94